M000272641

TABLE OF CONTENTS

Lighthouses are, by nature, romantic structures. They are watchtowers, where remote, lonely vigils are kept for fellow human beings traveling at sea - all honorable and noble duties. Lighthouses are also like the great transcontinental trains, whose use is waning, but about which there is much human drama.

Every lighthouse has associated with it facts, history, and lore, making each distinctive and unique, even if some are of the same design and utilize the same equipment. The story of each lighthouse can be thought of in terms of why it was needed, how it was built, the area and history that surrounded it, the lives of the keepers who maintained it and kept it operating, the arrival of great storms, the surrounding human events (from Seminole Wars to the Civil War to the Mariel Boat Lift), and, of course, the modern-day efforts at preservation.

In Florida, a sense of adventure is heightened not only by the history but the difficulty of construction. The value of something is always increased by the amount of human sweat that goes into it, and a lot of effort went into building Florida's lighthouses.

Building and maintaining a lighthouse in Florida, 100 or more years ago, when the land was a violent frontier, was an awesome challenge. The parts were transported long distances across a land fraught with dangers, such as warring Seminoles, or turbulent seas with mighty storms.

Several present-day lighthouses were erected with a unique design on reefs in the Keys. Some have pile-driven supports. The builders, designers, engineers, and workers lived some distance away. Bad weather caused frequent delays and put lives at peril. Florida's Keys in particular took the brunt of most Atlantic hurricanes that struck the United States, as they still do.

This book includes photographs and information on some lighthouses which have been largely undocumented. A decision was also made to include some of the minor lights, as these have, at times, been mentioned in various books, and it was felt that doing so would help explain the sometimes mysterious and dated references with modern data.

Unlike other books about Florida's lighthouses, this one has been organized in alphabetical order. The greatest advantage of this for readers is the ability to find a lighthouse quickly by name.

A general reference map on page 3, however, shows where the lighthouses are located about the state. Lighthouses which can be visited or easily viewed have their own reference maps to help locate them and to introduce the surrounding areas.

In present times, lighthouses are treasured historical monuments. Without human care, some of these valued links to the past could disappear. For example, in 2005, Cape St. George Lighthouse took a not-uncommon plunge into the sea.

Unfortunately, there seems to be a sort of divide between those who want to preserve the natural world and those wanting to save its human historical artifacts, perhaps because funds are so limited for acquisitions. Both types of preservationists should band together. After all, it is all Florida's heritage in danger of washing away in the population migration, subsequent development, and budget crunches.

LIGHTHOUSES AND LIGHTS

The earliest known lighthouse was the Pharos of Alexandria, and it was not short. Reportedly it was 350 feet in height, taller than any North American lighthouse. Like many later lighthouses, it was built of stone. The builders were Egyptians, and it was operational about 2300 years ago. It is also possible the gigantic Colossus of Rhodes was a lighthouse. When the Roman Empire overran the western world, it erected at least 30 lighthouses to guide its fleets. Alas, only the remnants of some of these ancient treasures still can be found

According to most historians, Boston Harbor Lighthouse, built in 1716, was the first in the United States, although Massachusetts was then a British colony. It is possible a tower at St. Augustine served as a lighthouse before that date. Lighthouse construction in the United States was so important a part of commerce that after the American Revolution the president personally appointed lighthouse keepers and kept a personal interest in lighthouse construction. A formal lighthouse organization was established in the 1850s. These duties eventually evolved to a United States Lighthouse Board, which was superseded in 1910 by a Bureau of Lighthouses. This was absorbed into the United States Coast Guard in 1939.

Lighthouse construction in Florida was most prolific in the 19th century, beginning when Florida was a territory, but apparently continues into the 21st century, with the newly-lighted Tierra Verde or Tampa Bay Watch Lighthouse.

For several thousand years, wood, coal, and coal oil was burned on platforms and in lighthouses to generate the light. Anyone who has had a coal stove knows the problems: coal blackens things with soot, and it is often hard on the lungs. Although candles and oil lamps were tried, some with reflectors about them, these were not very effective. The first revolution in lighting was Argand lamps, which burned various types of cleaner oils. The burning wicks of Argand lamps were round and hollow and within a half-shell-like reflector which boosted the light power.

At the turn of the 20th century, a system was invented for burning kerosene in the lighthouses. In modern times, many lighthouses, especially those at sea and unmanned, are powered by batteries, routinely changed by the Coast Guard, or by solar energy.

Among Florida lighthouses, a great number were lighted originally by a system known as Lewis lamps. These were an adaptation of the Argand lamps already in use with a reflector, and a lens. As with other oil systems, this one burned a wick. It also could have a number of lamps and reflectors placed in an array.

Fresnel lenses enabled a quantum leap in beam strength. The Fresnel lens provided a much brighter light and saved fuel, making the Lewis system obsolete. Light with the smallest Fresnel lenses was amplified more than 100 times over the best Lewis lamps.

Within the newly-invented (1822) Fresnel lenses, a focused array of ground and finely-polished glass prisms greatly increased capture of light from whatever source. In an age without plastic, the lenses were made by glass artisans and often resembled a work of art. Today's Fresnel lenses are plastic, but some of the older, glass lenses are still operating.

In time, lenses were built in different shapes for different results. Some devices were built to make the lenses rotate, casting a flashing beacon. Filters or colored glass could change the cast color, indeed could create different colors in different sectors, or angles from which the light was viewed.

While Fresnel lenses are still used, their light source is no longer burning oils or kerosene. Rather, the lights have been electrified. Many lighthouses are now lighted by modern optical devices.

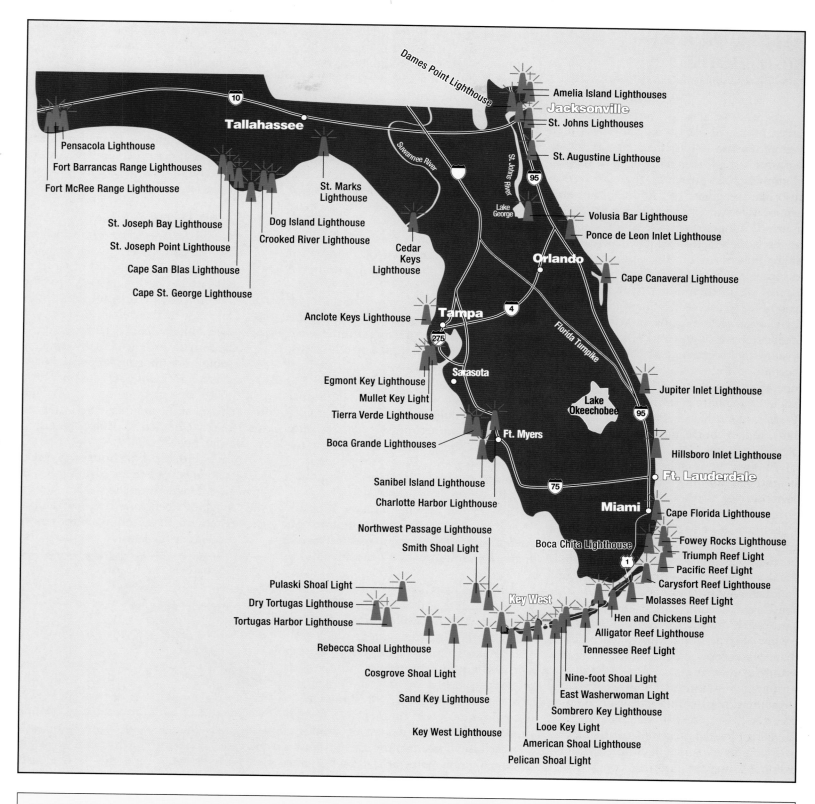

LIGHTHOUSE JARGON

Focal Plane. The focal plane is the height of the light above average mean sea level. Elevation affects focal plane, so if a lighthouse 100 feet tall is on a hill 20 feet above sea level, that lighthouse has a focal plane of 120 feet. Often, the beacon shines not from the exact top of the lighthouse, but from within a room a few feet below the top. This distance also must be considered in measuring the focal plane.

Fresnel Lens. A Fresnel lens is a series of prisms which focuses and concentrates the light of a beacon. It was developed by a Frenchman of the same name. Fresnel lenses come in seven orders. The first order is much larger and more powerful than a seventh. Each focuses the light into a beam. The special prisms in the center are described as "bull's eyes." Bull's-eye lenses are round, and look like a magnifying glass.

Lewis Lamps. A lighting system predating Fresnel lenses. This system was an American invention. The Lewis lamp added reflectors and lenses to the Argand lamp, an earlier technology consisting of an oil-burning beacon with a wick. The Argand lamp was devised by a Swiss.

Modern Optics. This refers to a range of newer lighting devices with a variety of trade names, such as Vega VRB-25 Beacon or Tidelands 300mm Beacon.

Lens Shapes. Some lenses are described by their shapes. A bivalve has two halves, like a clam shell. In fact, some lenses are called clam shells. Others are called drums, again a term describing their shape.

ALLIGATOR REEF LIGHTHOUSE
(Monroe County)

There are no alligators on Alligator Reef, nor is it shaped like an alligator. This reef and lighthouse were named after the USS *Alligator*, a ship that conducted a successful mission against pirates in the early 1800s and ran up onto the reef in 1822. The ship, destroyed by the crew abandoning it to keep it from falling into pirate hands, still lies on the shallow bottom. Both the wreck and the lighthouse are on the National Register of Historic Places. Most of the lighthouses located on offshore reefs in the Keys are named for wrecks. According to *Gulf Coast Lighthouses,* the lighthouse at Alligator reef is affectionately known as "Old Gator."

Top to bottom, this is a 150-foot lighthouse, with a focal plane (or plane of focus) of 136 feet (the official Coast Guard height of the light from mean high water). It is the second-highest lighthouse in overall physical height of the screw-pile design in the Keys. The highest is the Sombrero Key (also known as Sombrero Reef) Lighthouse at 156 feet. The pile of screw-piles has a screw on the bottom and is screwed into the reef.

Hurricanes, while frightening to those ashore, are monumental threats for those at a lighthouse or on a isolated island. While a boat can flee, lighthouses and islands can't. Land-side lighthouses allow occupants the option of moving to higher ground. Lighthouses built on reefs or on flat islands do not provide that luxury, particularly in the days before accurate forecasting and satellite imaging provided sufficient warning for evacuation. Radio did not come to reef lighthouses until a private donation connected four to the airwaves in 1931, these were one-way receivers. Given a choice of where to ride out a hurricane, most would opt for an island as opposed to a reef lighthouse. On an island, one still has something to grab - at least a palm tree or a hunk of land - if swept away. The closest thing to hold onto from Alligator Reef was land 2.5 miles away. On the other hand, a person on a screw-pile is likely safer because of how it is constructed and anchored than a person on any of the Keys in the event of most hurricanes.

Fate and surging high seas have carried more than one lighthouse keeper and sailor to their doom. Being hit by giant waves propelled at storm velocity is nearly unimaginable and probably feels like being hit with a brick wall. Sitting through 150+ mile-per-hour howling winds and surging surf for hours on end was surely a terrifying event sufficient to inspire urgent prayers from even the least devout. This happened at least three times at Alligator Reef Lighthouse (1919, 1935, and 1960).

Built in 1873 at a cost of $185,000, the lighthouse weathered the infamous Labor Day Hurricane of 1935, with winds gusting to 200-250 miles-per-hour, and seas surging to perhaps 30 or more feet above normal. More than 400 people died in the nearby area when waves rolled over the Keys. The number of dead is reported variously between 408 and 423. The 1935 hurricane was the first Category 5 to strike the US in recorded history and surpassed in fury the Category 4 hurricane of 1919, which had been described as the most powerful in the area, to that time.

Hurricane Donna swept through the area in 1960. Not quite as powerful as the Labor Day Hurricane, Donna never reached Category 5 (the most powerful) status, although it flickered close with sustained winds and still had gusts approaching 200 miles-per-hour. The Florida Lighthouse Association publication, *Florida Lighthouse Trail* (Pineapple Press), reports that lighthouse keepers lashed themselves to the structure to avoid being washed away by Hurricane Donna. Talk about riding out a storm!

Like all the reef lighthouses, Alligator Reef is not open to the public, but boaters putt around it and zoom up to it, fish about it, snorkel around it, and generally admire it.

Alligator Reef Lighthouse is officially described as an iron-pile platform of skeletal style with a white tower and a black watch room. The original lens was a first-order Fresnel. Some accounts describe it as a bivalve lens, but other lighthouse experts think it probably was not. A Fresnel is a type of lighting device designed by a Frenchman of that name, and bivalve simply means it has two halves. While the architect and manufacturer of the Fresnel lens are unknown, the builder was Paulding and Kemble of Cold Spring, New York.

The lighthouse is still active but presently lighted by a modern device known as a Vega VRB-25 Rotating Beacon. Vega is the manufacturer and an Australian company; VRB stands for variable rotating beacon. Many of Florida's operating lighthouses use or have used this make of beacon. The flashing light at Alligator Reef presently has two red sectors. Descriptions of light patterns in this book should not be used for navigation as they change from time to time.

DIRECTIONS

The lighthouse lies on the Atlantic side of US-1, a few miles off the coast of Islamorada, and 4 miles east of Indian Key and is visible from Matecumbe Key. Boat charters are available at Islamorada. Just to the south lies Indian Key State Historic Site, and a mile to the west of US-1 lies Lignumvitae Key Botanical State Park, both worthy visits. Under the docks of Islamorada are great numbers of tarpon, easily viewed by visitors. Considering the state lands, the lighthouse, and the tarpon, Islamorada is an excellent place to visit when in the Keys.

IMPORTANT DATES

1622   *Nuestra Senora del Rosario* Crashes onto Alligator Reef, Carrying a Lost Treasure of Gold and Silver

1822   USS *Alligator* Wrecks on Reef

1852   Daymark established

1857   Light House Board Recommends Construction

1870   Congress Authorizes Construction

1873   Lighthouse Lighted (November 25, 1873)

1919   The Great September Hurricane

1931   Radios Donated to Alligator Reef, American Shoal, Carysfort Reef, and Sombrero Key

1935   Labor Day Hurricane

1963   Lighthouse Automated

1980   Alligator Reef, American Shoal, and Sombrero Key Used as Outposts for Mariel Boat Lift

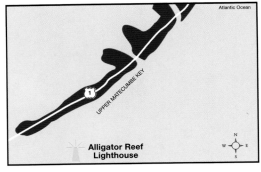

REEF LIGHTHOUSES

The Keys have six prominently-mentioned lighthouses built on reefs. They are Alligator Reef, American Shoal, Carysfort Reef, Fowey Rocks, Sand Key, and Sombrero Key (sometimes Sombrero Reef) Lighthouse. A seventh Keys lighthouse often mentioned in books is Rebecca Shoal Lighthouse, which no longer stands, but may yet again. In addition there are other shorter towers, which were never manned. Those towers are sometimes not considered to be lighthouses as they never had the "house" portion. Some of these lesser towers are included in this book.

Building on a reef, even in modern times, is not easy. The reef lighthouses were built in the 1800s under incredibly difficult conditions. The stories of each reef light's construction are individual sagas, often involving sunken supplies and building materials, delays due to funding problems and storms, and the peril of human life at sea, a place where we are, after all, intruders, and where giant, unanticipated storms come and small "pop-up cells" of bad weather can provide violent surprises.

Many of the reef lighthouses are known as screw-piles. This is because their feet were driven or screwed deep into the coral. In general, except for living quarters, the lighthouses were open, made of iron, described as skeletal (a bare skeleton), offering little wind resistance or resistance to storm-driven waves, thus better for weathering storms. Galvanization, which modern folks take for granted, was a new process when the reef lighthouses were being built out of iron.

Doors and windows could be swung open and locked into a open position allowing breezes to rip through. This provided natural air-conditioning, making for more comfortable quarters than on land. Also, rarely are mosquitoes (or any other bug) found at sea.

One problem is guano, or bird droppings, for nothing attracts sea birds more quickly than something that they can land on and fish from. At times guano has been harvested for fertilizer from constructed platforms at sea. Keeping guano out of drinking waters was also a concern for lighthouse keepers.

Lobsters and fish could supplement rations for keepers. This was important in a time of unpredictable transportation and re-supply from land.

Erecting the lights was a remarkable feat for the time, or any time for that matter. That the lighthouses have survived so many terrible storms is due to their special design.

BUILDING ON THE REEFS

Construction of lighthouses on coral reefs is an engineering feat requiring good weather, skill, and patience. Piles were driven or screwed-in first. On Alligator Reef, piles were driven ten feet into the coral. Driving a pile through dirt, say for a bridge, is a simple process, whacking away feet at a time, but passing through coral is not so easy. Coral, as anyone knows who has accidentally banged into it, is as hard as some rocks.

For Alligator Reef, the pile driver was 2.5 miles from shore. The pile hammer weighed 2,000 pounds, as much or more than some cars. The hammer blow fell an average distance of 18 feet to bang the piles, with each strike driving the pile from .5 inch to 1.5 inches at a time. Anyone who has witnessed a pile driver knows that a thunderous sound and resounding vibration travels great distances. Using an average push forward of an inch per strike, it took 120 whacks per pile, a force of 2,400,000 pounds (10 feet of the 26-foot length was driven into the coral). Once the piles were driven, parts were shipped from New York and assembled on the reef. And all this happened in the 1800s!

Opposite Page: **Alligator Reef Lighthouse** as seen from the air.

Left: **Alligator Reef Lighthouse was built to keep vessels from wrecking on the reef for which it was named.**

AMELIA ISLAND LIGHTHOUSE
(Nassau County)

Timucuan Indians held the area around Amelia Island when a handful of Spaniards and Frenchmen arrived in the New World to kill each other and compete for a giant land. The Spanish held Florida for three centuries, and the English held it but a relative few years (1763 to 1783). The name Amelia comes from English map makers. The English name stuck despite the relative insignificance of England in Florida history. The island was named for the daughter of English King George II, a tyrant; history has recorded little of the daughter. Amelia is, however, a beautiful name, and Amelia Island and its lighthouse are beautiful places.

In 1820, a lighthouse was established at Cumberland Island, Georgia, which is a substantial barrier island and presently a National Seashore with camping and accommodations at the famous Cumberland Inn. In 1839, this 60-foot Cumberland Island Lighthouse was moved stone by stone onto the new Florida portion of the United States at Amelia Island and erected brick by brick on a high (for the Sunshine State) hill. The height of this lighthouse is given variously in books and articles as 58, 59, 60, and 64 feet; believing that life should hold some mysteries, we will leave it at that (see box on lighthouse heights, this page). Its focal plane as seen from the sea is 107 feet. The mouth of the St. Marys River lies between the two islands of Cumberland and Amelia. In modern times, Trident submarines and sea kayaks pass through the area, along with more conventional craft.

The lighthouse marked the entrance to the St. Marys River. That river is a snaky 130 miles, and it is wide and usually deep up to Trader's Hill, Georgia, about 58 miles inland. It was used by sailing craft as a source of freshwater for early, seafaring explorers. Their boats left old ballast stones in the river, which can sometimes still be seen. After Trader's Hill, the river becomes increasingly twisty and shallow, so that at times it is difficult to push a kayak through. Brigands and renegades probably were well hidden once they got beyond Trader's Hill, for even today portions of the three prongs of the St. Marys River are wild and sometimes impenetrable places where bears and other wild creatures live.

By the 1800s, the St. Marys area was active with smuggling and slave running. Settlers were also arriving in the area, including inland around the Okefenokee Swamp, the source of the St. Marys (and the Suwannee River). The settlers were skirmishing with Creeks and Seminoles, basically one and the same. The Seminoles followed the same rituals, spoke the same languages, and earned their living in the same way as the Creeks. A series of forts was constructed, not only in the area around the St. Marys, but across all Florida to offer protection and enforce national policy. The Federal government sought sporadically and sometimes ineffectively to impose order on a disorderly frontier complete with slave trading, Indian attacks, and smuggling. The lighthouse, constructed to promote trade, also guided ships attempting to control the sprawling frontier.

On the eve of the Civil War, in 1858, the lighthouse was supplemented with one rear light and two front lights. The rear-range lighthouse used the smallest of Fresnel lens made, a sixth-order, sending forth a red light. The range lights disappeared during the Civil War. By aligning and sighting with these rear-range lights, a vessel could stay in the deepest, safest water. The use of these range lights was abandoned in 1899 for buoys, and the rear-range lights have since been destroyed. The lighthouse and its two front lights crossed, revealing the center of a channel between two shoals. Buoys better marked the safe path through the shoals, thus rendering nil the need for the rear and front lights.

The foundation is stone, the tower is brick. It's shape is described by the Coast Guard as conical. It has a white tower and a black lantern. The lens currently in the lighthouse is a third-order Fresnel. A similar lens once stood atop the Ponce de Leon Inlet Lighthouse. The original lighting was done with Lewis lights - 14 oil lamps with 15-inch reflectors. A third-order Fresnel lens was installed in 1856. A new third-Fresnel lens was installed in 1903. The light flashes every 10 seconds, and in the southeast appears red. The lighthouse is privately maintained.

The architect and builder of the Amelia Island Lighthouse was Winslow Lewis, and the original Fresnel lens was manufactured by Henri-LePuate, a French manufacturer. The second Fresnel lens was manufactured by Barbier & Benard, a French company.

DIRECTIONS

The lighthouse address on Fernandina Beach is 215 1/2 Lighthouse Circle. From I-95 north of Jacksonville, take A1A east onto Amelia Island. A1A will make a northerly turn and reach Atlantic Avenue. Turn to the east and the lighthouse will lie to the north on Lighthouse Circle.

IMPORTANT DATES

1820	Lighthouse Built at Cumberland Island
1821	Territory of Florida Becomes Part of the United States
1838-9	Lighthouse Moved to Amelia Island
1839	Lighthouse First Lighted
1856	Third-order Fresnel Lens Operational
1858	North Rear-Range Lights Added
1861	Lights Hidden, Civil War
1867	Light Reestablished After Civil War
1871	North Range Lights Rebuilt
1899	North Range Lights Use Stopped
1903	New Third-order Fresnel Lens Installed
1933	Light Electrified

LIGHTHOUSE HEIGHTS

Why do lighthouse heights vary so greatly in popular books? It is because of different methods of determining the height.

A lands man would measure the tower. That is from the ground to its tippy top. Unfortunately, the top might be a lightning rod or a vent ball. Vent balls were often needed because of the heat generated by lighting.

A mariner needs to know exactly how high is the beacon. The mariner would use a sextant to determine the angle. Sextants measure angles and sailors need to know the height of the light to determine the distance.

Because of the curvature of the earth, the light vanishes at a certain point. There is a "loom" from the light after it vanishes. (Loom is derived from illumination.)

The highest focal plane (191 feet) in Florida belongs to the Pensacola light while the tallest lighthouse tower is Ponce de Leon Inlet (175 feet).

The Coast Guard prepares and the Government Printing Office publishes a Light List. Height in that report is defined as the distance from mean high water to the focal plane of the light. This often yields a different height than those in popular print, but one that means something to seamen.

ELECTRIFICATION

The oldest lighthouses existed in the times before the modern use of electricity, a mysterious force we all take for granted in today's world. Old power sources of burning whale oils and kerosene have been replaced with juice from the local utility. Lighthouses at sea, however, are often supplied by battery-powered equipment, usually solar powered.

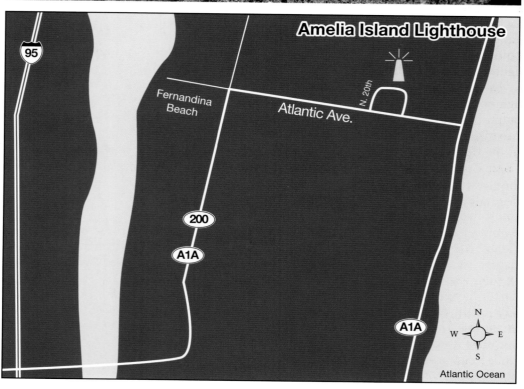

Above, left: Amelia Island Lighthouse was built to help guide vessels into the St. Mary's River.

Above, right: An aerial view of Amelia Island Lighthouse.

Above: The lens in Amelia Island Lighthouse.

Opposite page: Historic photo of Amelia Island North Range Light circa 1872-1880.

AMERICAN SHOAL LIGHTHOUSE
(Monroe County)

One of the wrecks more widely-known in the Keys is that of HMS *Loo*, an English frigate that crashed into coral in 1744. It is from a corruption of Loo that the Looe Key and Looe Reef have been given their names. When pronounced, the "e" is silent. American Shoal Lighthouse was originally to have been located at Looe Key.

When the *Loo* wrecked, it was not alone. Another boat, *Billander Betty,* accompanying the *Loo,* likewise struck the coral. Both boats were stuck, and the crew used smaller vessels to reach safety. The captain of the *Loo* was court-martialed but acquitted of dereliction.

Located east of Sugarloaf Key and north of Key West, this 109-foot lighthouse went into service on July 15, 1880. The placing of a lighthouse on American Shoal was a culmination of more than 50 years of efforts.

In 1826, a modest brick, 30-foot-tall beacon was built on Looe Key. It lasted only seven years, until a hurricane took it down in 1833. In 1850, a Looe daymark (an unlighted marker) was erected, and a daymark was placed on American Shoal in 1852. The daymarks were better than nothing for preventing wrecks, but not as good as a lighthouse.

American Shoal Lighthouse was built at a cost of $125,000 more or less at the same time as Fowey Rocks Lighthouse and is of the same design with a few tweaks. The two lighthouses were painted different colors to avoid confusing mariners. The lights of both American Shoal and Fowey Rocks Lighthouses have red sectors warning of dangerous shoals. American Shoal Lighthouse is considered the last manned reef lighthouse built in the Florida Keys.

In addition to warning mariners, lighthouses have at times served as remote outposts. Like the Alligator Reef Lighthouse, American Shoal Lighthouse played a role in the Cuban or Mariel Boat Lift of 1980. Coast Guard personnel at the lighthouses monitored the flow of refugees escaping from the poor Communist country and land of sugarcane to the south.

In 1990, an image of American Shoal Lighthouse was represented on a 25-cent stamp issued by the United States Postal Service. On that stamp, a Coast Guard cutter is passing or approaching the lighthouse, and the keeper's quarters are bright red. The bright red is factual enough but not the cutter. It should be noted that while a cutter approaches the lighthouse on a stamp, this could not happen because the water is too shallow. This stamp is part of a commemorative lighthouse series.

Made of iron, this screw-pile lighthouse is described by the Coast Guard as a skeletal, octagonal pyramid. The original lens was a first-order Fresnel of a "beehive" shape. It is presently lighted by a Vega VRB-25 Beacon. The light flashes white at 15-second intervals and has two red sectors. The builder was Phoenix Iron Company of Trenton, New Jersey. The Fresnel lens was built by Henri-LePaute in 1874. The architect is unknown.

A report posted on the website of Lighthousefriends.com suggests American Shoal was named for the vessel *America*, a ship, which the website says, sank while carrying blocks to Fort Jefferson in the Dry Tortugas. However, the *America* was bound from New York to Mobile when it sank.

DIRECTIONS

It is located approximately 6.5 miles to the south of Sugarloaf Key and can be seen from Sugarloaf.

IMPORTANT DATES

1744	Wreck of HMS *Loo*
1826	Brick Beacon Built at Looe Key
1833	Looe Key Tower Collapses in Hurricane
1850	Daymark Constructed at Looe Key
1852	Daymark Constructed at American Shoal
1876	Lighthouse Board Proposes Construction
1878	Lighthouse Construction Begun
1880	Lighthouse Lighted (July 15)
1912	Incandescent Oil Vapor Lamp Used
1931	Radios Donated to Alligator Reef, American Shoal, Carysfort Reef, and Sombrero Key
1963	Lighthouse Automated
1980	Alligator Reef, American Shoal, and Sombrero Key Used as Outposts During Mariel Boat Lift
1990	American Shoal Postage Stamp Issued

FRESNEL LENSES

Upon reading one of the longest and greatest novels ever written, Les Miserables by Victor Hugo, the author wanted to relay the adventures of the hero Jean Valjean. Naturally, the American author mispronounced this as "Gene Valgene," rhyming with Vaseline, and was quickly corrected as a bumpkin by someone who saw the musical Les Miserables in the comfort of a theater in a few hours rather than spending five days digesting 1,400 pages of book. It is "John Valjohn," or, better yet, "Zhon Val-zhon." Likewise, to avoid being a bumpkin about the Fresnel lens, it is better to not pronounce it like the city of Fresno, California, but call it fray-nel, in the French fashion.

Augustin Jean (John) Fresnel was a Frenchman who lived during the time of Napoleon. In 1822, he invented the system called the Fresnel lens. By efficiently focusing and refracting light, his lens design produced a much more powerful light than the system then in use. Early Fresnel lenses were lighted by fuels before the coming of electricity.

There are six orders or magnitudes of Fresnel lenses, with sixth being the weakest and first being the most powerful. At sea, the most powerful order will be visible for the longest distance. So much power may not be needed, however, within small harbors and bays. A 3.5-order Fresnel has been used in Florida, for example at Boca Grande.

Fresnel lenses can weigh up to 3 tons. A first-order lens can have more than 1,000 glass parts and looks like (and is) a work of art.

HURRICANES AND TROPICAL STORMS

Hurricanes are violent storms formed by low-pressure areas revolving around a center of even-lower pressure. The revolution is counter-clockwise in the Northern Hemisphere and clockwise in the Southern. The minimum sustained wind speed such a low-pressure system must maintain to be considered a hurricane is 74 miles-per-hour, which is considered a Category 1 hurricane. The weakest is a Category 1. The most powerful is a Category 5. The center around which the hurricane rotates is called the eye, and the average size of an eye is 14 miles in diameter. Here are the sustained wind speeds from the Saffir/Simpson Classification Scale:

Tropical Storm 39-73 miles-per-hour
Category 1 74-95 miles-per-hour
Category 2 96-110 miles-per-hour
Category 3 111-130 miles-per-hour
Category 4 131-155 miles-per-hour
Category 5 156+ miles-per-hour

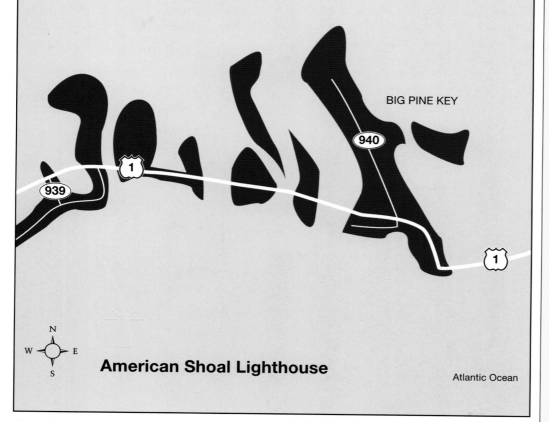

American Shoal Lighthouse

BIG PINE KEY

Atlantic Ocean

ORDER IN THE LIGHTHOUSE

Fresnel lenses vary from those taller than most basketball players to those small enough to fit in the trunk of your car. The earliest Fresnel lenses came in seven orders without variation. The distance from the flame to the lens determined the order, which in turn determined the size. The orders are: first, second, third, third and-a-half, fourth, fifth, and sixth.

The height varied from 7 feet 10 inches for a first-order Fresnel lens to 1 foot 5 inches for a sixth order. A first-order Fresnel has an inner diameter of 6 feet 1 inch to go with its massive height, and when made out of so many glass prisms and housing, has a substantial weight.

Different lenses had different purposes. A sixth-order Fresnel might sit in a smaller lighthouse on a breakwater. A third-and-a-half order Fresnel would be appropriate as a harbor light. First-order Fresnel lenses were needed in areas like the Keys to warn away boats from a great distance.

Opposite Page and Top: Views of American Shoal Lighthouse. This lighthouse was built to prevent wrecks on American Shoal and nearby Looe Reef.

ANCLOTE KEYS LIGHTHOUSE
(Pinellas and Pasco counties)

The effort to preserve the lighthouse on Anclote Key is a remarkable success story. Dedicated work of local citizens plus enlightened thinking on the part of the state have resulted in the lighthouse being resurrected from decades of neglect and vandalism. As of this writing, a permanent residence has been established on the island for a park ranger and a shuttle service is in the foreseeable future, perhaps between the island and Tarpon Springs. It may, in fact, exist by publication. In October 2005, the lighthouse was opened for a tour on one weekend of the month, with hopes of continuing this in the future. A replica Fresnel lens was operating, casting a beam 16 to 17 miles, with flashes at 30-second intervals.

Originally the state established Anclote Key State Preserve, since designated a state park, and now part of a Gulf Geo-park. This entity includes Egmont Key (with another, less spectacular lighthouse), Caledesi Island State Park, and other public lands.

Like Boca Grande, the lighthouse sits on a island that is bi-county. County lines bisect the island, not at all equally, so that while the lighthouse lies in Pinellas County, the majority of the island lies in Pasco.

There are four main barrier islands in the Anclote Keys. Anclote Key is the longest, stretching south to north 3 miles. To the east lies Dutchman Key. To the north are North Anclote Key and North Key. There are also smaller smidgens of land and spoil islands. The lighthouse, called in print both Anclote Key and Anclote Keys Lighthouse, is one and the same thing.

Key comes from the Spanish word *Cayo*, for barrier island, while Anclote is Spanish word of debated meaning. Some say it means safe harbor. Thus it is the island of safe harbor. Others say it means anchor or grapple. When the current is ripping, a boater may have a hard time anchoring at Anclote or keeping a boat from stranding as the rapidly receding tide goes out.

A winding boardwalk leads perhaps a quarter mile to where the lighthouse stands towering over everything on a flat, low island. The boardwalk crosses a tidal pool.

In the Coast Guard 1983 Light List, the last list when the light was in service, the Coast Guard height from mean high water to the focal plane was 101 feet. Other heights are given in popular books.

Beside the lighthouse, when visited in 2005, an osprey carrying a fish in its talons landed in its nest in a tall tree. It was a male osprey bringing a snack to his mate and perhaps brood. He quickly flew off again, perhaps to feed himself, while the female looked down from her massive nest on the flightless humans below.

Set on pilings, the lighthouse is cast iron, of a skeletal shape with a central cylinder, and built at a cost of $35,000. It was brown with a black lantern. The third-order Fresnel lens originally sent four grouped white flashes out every 30 seconds. In 1899, this sequence was changed to one red flash every 30 seconds. The modern optic is a fourth-order Fresnel which flashes white. While the architect and builder are unknown, the original Fresnel lens was built by Henri-LePaute.

DIRECTIONS

It is possible to kayak 3 miles to Anclote from Howard Park in Tarpon Springs with proper precautions and assuming one is a better than average kayaker and the weather is not too bad. Primitive camping is allowed on the north end of the island.

Howard Park is prominently announced by signs along Alternate-19 in Tarpon Springs. Visitors should see the sponge docks in Tarpon Springs. The Anclote Keys Lighthouse allowed Tarpon Springs' economy to boom.

The sponge divers in Tarpon Springs were largely of Greek descent. A Greek Orthodox Church is located in the city, and on January 6 of each year, The Feast of (or The Holy Day of) Epiphany is celebrated in a unique way. A cross, blessed by a priest, is tossed into Spring Bayou, and Greek youths dive in and compete to recover the cross. The victor is blessed with a year of good luck. The 2006 Epiphany was the centennial, and a celebration was held from January 4 to 8.

IMPORTANT DATES

1876	Tarpon Springs Settled
1887	Lighthouse Lit (September 15)
1907	Tarpon Springs Sponge Exchange Created
1952	Automated
1963	Electrified
1985	Lighthouse Deactivated
2003	Lighthouse Re-lighted
2004	Replica Fourth-Order Fresnel Lens Installed
2006	Centennial Epiphany Celebration

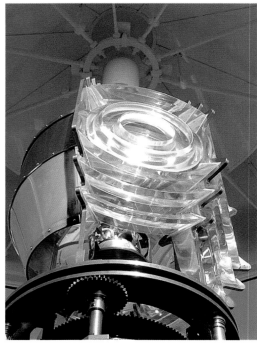

Above: The fourth-order Fresnel lens.

Opposite Page, top, left: Approaching Anclote Key Lighthouse, an osprey nest can be seen at the top of a dead tree. This view of the lighthouse is before restoration was complete.

Bottom, left: Visitors exit a shuttle boat.

Top, right: A view of the walk from the boat landing as seen from the lighthouse.

Middle, right: The visitors center.

Bottom, right: An early lighthouse in the Anclote River.

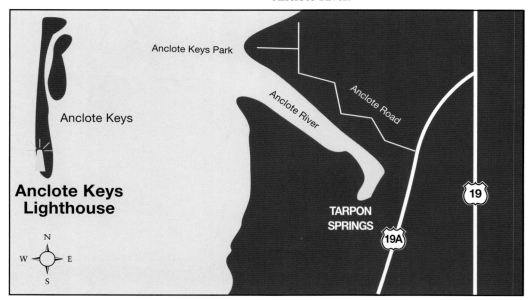

Anclote Keys Park

Anclote River

Anclote Road

Anclote Keys

Anclote Keys Lighthouse

TARPON SPRINGS

19

19A

N / W E / S

BOCA CHITA LIGHTHOUSE
(Dade County)

The Boca Chita Lighthouse is not in the Coast Guard domain and wasn't publicly constructed. It is, nonetheless, a remarkable structure and, in most other ways a lighthouse. It is included in this book because most people interested in Florida lighthouses would be interested in knowing about it.

There is debate about whether Boca Chita was ever lighted, although it is possible it was built (by a very successful business titan) as a beacon for him and his island guests. It was a private lighthouse owned by Mark C. Honeywell and designed by the prominent Miami architectural firm of August Geiger. At one time Honeywell owned the island, 29 acres in the Atlantic Ocean, so small it does not appear on DeLorme's *Florida's Atlas and Gazetteer*.

Geiger was responsible for an impressive number of architectural marvels, including The Lincoln Hotel on Miami Beach and several Dade County schools. A list of his works can be viewed on the park website by accessing:

http//www.nps.bisc/resource/cultural/bihistoricresourcestudy.pdf.

A popular tale about the lighthouse says that when it was lighted, the Coast Guard shut it down. This legend goes that the Coast Guard determined it not an approved aid to navigation and thus potentially confusing. Supposedly Honeywell was furious, as might befit a captain of industry thwarted by government. However, park resources point out that there are no fixtures in the lantern room for mounting a light of any sort, nor does it appear there ever were any.

THE VIEW FROM THE WATER

Florida's lighthouses exist for three primary purposes: to warn vessels off dangerous reefs and shoals, to guide boats into harbor, and to tell mariners where they are. All lighthouses are intended to avoid stranding or running aground. Lights at Boca Grande, for example, help pilots stay in the deepest water. By aligning the front and rear-range lights, captains can be sure of their position in the channel.

HB

BIG PINE SHOAL LIGHT
(Monroe County)

Big Pine Shoal Light is located on the seaward edge of the reef of the same name. At present, it is 16 feet high on a dolphin and flashes red every 2.5 seconds.

The term "light" is used to identify it and other towers in this book which were designed to operate unmanned. Many such structures existed and some still exist as aids to navigation. About a dozen are mentioned in this book.

This light is atop a dolphin, a form of lighthouse construction something like a teepee. There are several piles tied together at the top.

This is a lettered marker, rare in the United States. Lettered markers indicate safe water with no lateral significance. For instance, if a lettered marker SJ were placed at the seaward end of the shipping channel into the St. Johns River, a vessel could pass on either side of the marker and not run aground. Lateral aids to navigation would guide the mariner in the channel, with red aids on the right side when returning from sea (thus red, right returning).

Left: Big Pine Shoal Light serves both to mark the shoal and to help the mariner stay in the channel. This early photo is probably from the 1930's or 1940s.

Opposite Page: Constructed for tycoon Mark Honeywell, beautiful Boca Chita Lighthouse was ornamental and never aided navigation.

Mark Honeywell was the founder of the very large Honeywell company, which currently employs around 90,000 people. The company originally was involved in automatic controls, heating systems, and thermostats, but now is involved in many types of business, such as home security, and is an aerospace and defense contractor.

A number of structures, including the lighthouse, were built on the island for Honeywell between 1937 and 1940. The Boca Chita Historic District has been nominated to The National Register of Historic Places. All of the structures have been built of oolitic limestone, limestone rock containing round or egg-shaped bodies.

As the park internet literature points out, oolitic limestone is great for weathering hurricanes. For over six decades, the lighthouse and structures have survived storm surges and high winds. In August 1992, Category 5 Hurricane Andrew ran over nearby Fowey Rocks with winds clocked at 169 miles-per-hour, and the lighthouse survived.

Like Fowey Rocks Lighthouse, Boca Chita lies within Biscayne National Park. Over 40 islands and 173,000 acres (mostly in the water) are within the park, which is one of the jewels of the National Park Service.

Unlike the Coast Guard maintained offshore lighthouses, Boca Chita is open to the public for tours during parts of the year, and whenever park service personnel are on the island, the lighthouse is open to the public. A local concession provides boat transportation to the island.

There is a brutal mosquito season on the islands. National parks do not spray malathion or other pesticides into the world. Sane travelers usually stay away from the islands during the warmer months and wait for the first cold snap to lay the little pests low.

No one appears certain of the height of the lighthouse. No figures are given in park literature. Management of Biscayne National Park estimates the height to be 65 feet.

DIRECTIONS

It is 9 miles to Boca Chita from the mainland. Independent boaters would do well to be familiar with the area or study charts. It is a longer haul north beyond Boca Chita to Fowey Rocks, which is located 4 miles from the tiny island of Soldier Key, a dot on the *Gazetteer*. Biscayne National Park, to the east of Homestead in Dade County, can be accessed from US-1 or the Florida Turnpike. The National Park Center is at Convoy Point, east of Homestead.

CAPE CANAVERAL LIGHTHOUSE
(Brevard County)

Some people mistakenly believe the Cape Canaveral Lighthouse is at Kennedy Space Center. It is not. Rather, it is located on Cape Canaveral Air Force Station. Some folks then mistakenly think it is Cape Canaveral Air Force Base, as "station" is a term normally associated with the Navy. Kennedy Space Center actually is located on Merritt Island, Florida, west of Cape Canaveral Air Force Station.

Visitors to Cape Canaveral will usually pass by the lighthouse while on a bus tour but may not even get the chance to stop and photograph the structure. However, the lighthouse can be visited by group tours arranged in advance by contacting the station.

Of the three names this area is known by, perhaps the first is the most appropriate and least known. In the 1600s, Spanish explorer Ponce de Leon gave the area the name of *Caba de las Corrientes,* Cape of the Currents, indicating the need for a lighthouse.

Canaveral, is not an actual Spanish word, but it is a term that linguists say means a place of either cane or roots. Logically such a term could be associated with mangroves (for their roots), which are in their northern range in this area, or saltmarsh grasses (which often look like cane).

The third name was given to this area after President Kennedy was assassinated in 1963. The home of the space program was renamed by executive order in Kennedy's honor by his successor, Lyndon Johnson, and remained Cape Kennedy for ten years. The missile range is known as the Eastern Missile Range and is owned, maintained, and operated by the 45th Space Wing at Patrick Air Force Base and Cape Canaveral Air Force Station. It was Kennedy, of course, who proclaimed the landing of a man on the Moon as a national goal.

Some people didn't like this change. In 1973, the name of Cape Canaveral was restored by an act of the Florida legislature. It remains property of the United States Air Force. The cape is now Cape Canaveral and probably will be forever.

The first lighthouse at the Cape was erected during 1848, three years after Florida became a state and prior to the Civil War. Beginning in the 1830s and up to the Civil War, lighthouse building went on at a pace never equaled again. This was possible, in part, because Florida became a United States Territory in 1821.

The first lighthouse at Cape Canaveral was too short and not bright enough. It stood 60 feet. Despite 15 lamps with 21-inch reflectors, boats couldn't see it until they had already wrecked on The Southeast Shoals.

For a time, the lighthouse was abandoned because of warring Seminoles. In 1850, the lighthouse keeper fled from the Seminoles, as would any sane person left alone with warriors in the area.

Service was again interrupted at the beginning of the Civil War, when the Secretary of the Confederate Navy, Mr. Stephen R. Mallory, of Pensacola, ordered that all the lighthouses on the southern coasts be discontinued. Word to that effect was transmitted to Captain Burnham, through Captain Drummit, the Collector of Port Taxes of New Smryna, whereupon Burnham dismantled the works by carefully taking down the lamps and clockwork, and packing them in wood crates, which were buried in Burnham's orange grove for safe keeping. After the war ended in 1865, Burnham turned this material over to the government officials in good order and was highly commended for his faithful care of government property. The lamps were never replaced on the tower because the government had, just prior to the war, appropriated the substantial sum of $136,000 for a new lighthouse.

Shortly after the Civil War, the new iron lighthouse was completed in 1868. It was fitted with a new lamp and clock mechanism. This lighthouse stood 151 feet tall and the light was now high enough to be effective. The Coast Guard height from average high tide to the focal plane is 137 feet. The original lighthouse was only 60 feet tall. The two lighthouses stood side by side until 1892.

The new lighthouse stood in its original location for 26 years. When erosion threatened the lighthouse, it was moved to the the present site between 1892-94.

The lighthouse has been part of Canaveral Air Force Station since the station was created following World War II, and it is currently illuminated by a rotating searchlight, officially described as a DCB-224, which emits a white flash twice every 20 seconds. The distinctive black-and-white stripes daymark the iron-and-brick structure. The architect is unknown, but the structure was built by West Point Foundry, on the other side of the river from West Point, New York, and the original first-order Fresnel lens was made by Henri-LePaute and is on display at the Ponce de Leon Inlet Lighthouse.

From US-1 along the mainland coast, there are several bridges east to Merritt Island (home of a National Wildlife Refuge) and then to Canaveral. SR-520 and SR-528 are probably the best. Between the two islands lies the Banana River, which despite its name, is not a river at all, but a sort of lagoon. The waterway between the mainland and Merritt Island is called the Indian River.

Climbing up lighthouse stairways is not for the claustrophobic or those with vertigo. Generally, only the first three levels are open to the public, but they are sufficiently tight to make climbers cautious. The rooms on the second and third floor were to have housed the lighthouse keepers, but it is reported that bugs and heat drove them to more comfortable living arrangements in buildings outside the lighthouse.

DIRECTIONS

From US-1 north of Cocoa, go east on SR-528. Make an immediate north turn on SR-401 after crossing the Banana River. If this turn is missed, SR-528 will eventually lead to A1A which goes south down the beach to Patrick Air Force Base.

Sonny Witt is the Deputy Commander of the Cape Canaveral Air Force Station. Deputy Commanders are usually colonels or generals. Sonny Witt is a civilian. Having a civilian deputy commander is believed to provide continuity in the military, where there are frequent changes of command.

There are fantastic beaches nearby at Canaveral National Seashore, where it is possible to walk 24 uninterrupted miles while listening to the surf. Adjoining is the Merritt Island National Wildlife Refuge. The two provide almost 200,000 acres of wildlife viewing, hiking, and nature education. The area is popular for "surf" kayaking as well as traditional kayaking in lagoons, saltmarsh, and along the Intracoastal. Kennedy Space Center is also a great educational visit.

Beginning June 14, 2006, the 45th Space Wing began to offer free tours of the lighthouse on the second Wednesday of every month. It is hoped that these will be successful and continue. It is necessary to call in advance and to make reservations. The phone number is in Appendix A under Cape Canaveral Lighthouse Foundation. A gift shop now operates within the lighthouse when it is open and is staffed by volunteers.

IMPORTANT DATES

1848 First Lighthouse
1850 Abandoned Because of Threats from Seminoles
1868 Second Lighthouse
1893 Lighthouse Moved
1894 Second Lighthouse Re-lighted
1960 Automated
1963 Re-named Cape Kennedy
1973 Re-named Cape Canaveral

SB

FAREWELL TO A SPECIES

Connecting the Kennedy Space Center with Disney World was thought to be a great idea for tourism and it was. But it also drove a road straight through a marsh containing the last wild population of dusky seaside sparrows. Some scientists quibble about whether this was a species or a sub-species. To save the population from total extinction, a captive-breeding program was established and birds were captured in the wild. Only one problem. Only male birds were captured. Orange Band, the last dusky seaside sparrow male, died on June 18, 1987.

CANAVERAL'S KEEPER

In July of 1853, Captain Mills O. Burham was appointed lighthouse keeper for Cape Canaveral Lighthouse. He was the third keeper. Formerly he had traded in turtles and raised pineapples near Vero Beach. For the next 33 years, until his death in 1886, he served continuously as the lighthouse keeper. It was a lighthouse-keeping family. His wife Mary assisted him, not an uncommon practice, and his oldest daughter Frances was an assistant lighthouse keeper. Captain and Mrs. Burham are buried on Cape Canaveral in a family cemetery. It is believed that his relatives served as keepers into the 20th century.

Top: Majestic Cape Canaveral Lighthouse serves to warn mariners of dangerous shoals.

Bottom: The bottom of the stairwell up Cape Canaveral Lighthouse leads to quarters on the second and third floors.

SB

CAPE FLORIDA LIGHTHOUSE
(Dade County)

Cape Florida Lighthouse can be thought of in terms of shipwrecks, warring Seminoles, the beach at a first-class state park, and Hurricane Andrew, which came straight at it as a Category 4 or 5 hurricane.

The initial contract for building the lighthouse was awarded to a Samuel Lincoln of Boston in April of 1824. In August of that year, the first ship of materials sank with no survivors. A Noah Humphreys of Hingham, Massachusetts, was given the next contract. His boat delivered the materials safely.

History books generally record three Seminole Wars in the early 1800s. In reality, there was one long series of skirmishes, perhaps stretching 60-70 years, with lulls of fatigue or peace - take your pick. Each time there was a truce, some new outrage caused the Seminoles to attack, and their attacks were often brutal. Settlers and soldiers responded with long, protracted searches for the Seminoles and likewise brutal acts in the rare event Seminoles were actually found. Many Native Americans, like Osceola, could only be captured by duping them with flags of truce then taking them captive. Andrew Jackson, for whom Jacksonville was named, earned a reputation as an "Indian fighter" largely at the expense of Seminoles and Creeks, essentially the same people. (Jackson invaded Florida in 1818, forcing Spain to cede the land to the United States.) Not only were the Seminoles pretty good at hiding and familiar with the land, but those searching for them were often a little inept, sometimes settling for shooting peaceful Seminoles when the marauding ones could not be found.

The original Cape Florida lighthouse, built in 1825, was attacked and burned by Seminoles in 1836 during the Second Seminole War. Before the attack at Cape Florida, the settlers in the area had left, leaving behind two men, one keeper and a man who was probably an African-American slave. In January 1836, the Cooley family was massacred near Fort Lauderdale on New River, sparking this exodus to Key West. Only five days before the attack, John Dubose, the Lighthouse keeper, left for Key West to celebrate his birthday, leaving John Thompson, who wrote a first-person account of the ensuing siege, and Aaron Carter, the probable slave.

It is only by a leap of imagination that we visualize the conditions during the attack. No electricity. No road. No telephone. No 911. No friendly faces for miles. According to some reports, more than 40 Seminoles pressed the attack on a hot July day. Two men alone faced an enemy intent on their death. Thompson used every means at hand while defending his life, the slave, and the lighthouse. The Seminoles set the lighthouse door on fire. This fire was enhanced by lamp oil, 225 gallons of it. Flames spread to the wooden portions of the lighthouse, driving the two keepers upward.

In Thompson's own words -

One the 23d of July last, as I was going from the kitchen to the dwelling house, I discovered a large body of Indians within 25 yards of me, back of the kitchen. I ran for the lighthouse and called out to the old Negro man that was with me to run, for the Indians were near. At that moment, they discharged a volley of rifle balls, which cut my clothes and hat and perforated the door in many places.

We got in, and as I was turning the key, the savages had hold of the door. I stationed the Negro at the door, with orders to let me know if they attempted to break in. Then I took my three muskets, which were loaded with ball and buckshot, and went to the second window. Seeing a large body of them opposite the dwelling house, I discharged my muskets in succession among them, which put them in some confusion.

For the second time, they began their horrid yells....I fired at them from some other windows and from the top of the lighthouse; in fact, I fired whenever I could get an Indian for a mark. I kept them from the lighthouse until dark.

They then poured in a heavy fire at all the windows and lantern. That was the time they set fire to the door...the flames spread fast, being fed with yellow pine wood. Their balls had perforated the tin tanks of oil...my bedding, clothing....everything I had was soaked in oil. I stopped at the door until driven away by the flames.

I took a keg of gunpowder, my balls, and one musket to the top...then went below and began to cut away the stairs...I had difficulty getting the old Negro up the space...the flames now drove me from my labor, and I retreated to the top of the house...

At last the awful moment arrived: the cracking flames burnt around me. The savages at the same time began their hellish yells. My poor old Negro looked to me with tears in his eyes, but could not speak. We went out of the lantern and lay down on the edge of the platform, two feet wide.

The lantern now was full of flame and the lamps and glasses were bursting and flying in all directions. My clothes were on fire, but to move from the place where I was would be instant death from their rifles. My flesh was roasting.

To put an end to my horrible suffering, I got up and threw the keg of gunpowder down the scuttle. It exploded instantly and shook the tower from top to bottom...

The Negro man said he was wounded, which was the last word he spoke...."

That loud explosion summoned two nearby boats (the US Navy Transport Schooner *Motto* and the Sloop of War *Concord*), whose crews saved the life of the lighthouse keeper.

The next morning....

I thought I could see a vessel not far off. I took a piece of the old Negro's trousers that had escaped the flames by being wet with blood, and made a signal.

It took yet another day to take the badly burned and wounded Thompson down from the top of the lighthouse where he lay suffering.

The attack was successful in the sense that it closed the lighthouse. A new lighthouse was funded in 1837, and Winslow Lewis was given the contract. When the ship arrived, it found the area in the hands of hostile Native Americans. The contract was rescinded and a new beacon delayed almost a decade. An attempt at rebuilding was stifled in 1841 by construction problems. In 1846, construction began again, and this time it was successful. The light was re-lighted in 1847 and improved in 1855. During the improvements, the height was raised from 65 to 95 or 96 feet (96 is the height the state park gives), and a fixed, second-order Fresnel lens was installed. Confederate sympathizers smashed the lens' central prism and the reflector in August of 1861.

Re-lighted in 1866, the Fresnel lens was removed and sent to a depot at Staten Island, New York, when Fowey Rocks Lighthouse became operational in 1878. Fowey Rocks Lighthouse was built because the Cape Florida Lighthouse did not seem to prevent wrecks in the area.

Sometime between 1968-70, a drum lens was installed. The Coast Guard re-lighted the light on July Fourth, Independence Day, 1978. Of brick, iron, and granite construction, the lighthouse was deactivated again in 1987.

In August 1992, intense and powerful Hurricane Andrew ran right over the State Park. The hurricane snapped and felled trees in and around Homestead, Miami, and the Everglades. While Andrew caused only minimal damage to the lighthouse and keeper's dwelling (it destroyed the porch, and there was water damage), the plentiful Australian pines covering almost all the grounds were battered. As a result of the storm, a project was funded to remove exotic vegetation. The remaining pines were removed, significantly changing the look of the island. Australian "pine" is really not in

ss

the pine family and is a common name for three species of invasive trees which change the native vegetation by their presence.

In 2005, the United States National Park Service Underground Railroad Network to Freedom admitted Bill Baggs Cape Florida State Park. This is based on conclusive historical evidence based on first-hand accounts of escaped slaves and Seminoles with African descent passing through the area and onto Andros in the Bahamas. Information is available on the state park website. See Appendix A for park contacts.

The lighthouse is presently in operation using a 250-mm plastic Fresnel lens, with a 75-watt light. The light pattern is 1 second on, 5 seconds off. Cape Florida is an aid to navigation, but the primary, seacoast, navigational beacon in the area remains Fowey Rocks.

In appearance, Cape Florida Lighthouse is described as a conical brick tower, white, with a black lantern. While the architect is unknown, it may have been Winslow Lewis, who built it with Leonard Hammond. George Meade oversaw the work to heighten the tower, which included a new lantern room. The lighthouse was originally lighted with Lewis lamps, and the subsequent Fresnel lens was made by Henri-LePaute.

The restored lighthouse is on the National Register of Historic Sites and sits on the southerly tip of Bill Baggs Cape Florida State Park. The park is named for an editor of the *Miami Herald* who was an ardent environmentalist. It is said to be the oldest structure still standing in South Florida. The park is very busy and attracts an average of 850,000 visitors annually. The Lighthouse Cafe, which burned down in 2004, is being rebuilt, and will likely be finished by publication of this book. In the meantime, the Boaters Grill serves food at No Name Harbor within the park. A concession rents bikes, blades, and kayaks. Or a visitor can just lie on a blanket spread on the sand and soak up the sun between dips.

DIRECTIONS

To reach the park (formerly designated a state recreation area), go south of Miami on US-1 and turn east on Rickenbacker Causeway. Follow Crandon Boulevard, a continuation of the causeway, south to the park.

At present, guided tours of the lighthouse are given Thursday thru Monday at 10:00 AM and 1:00 PM.

www.floridastateparks.org/capeflorida/ParkSummary.cfm

IMPORTANT DATES

1822	Congress Approves Funds for Lighthouse
1824	Additional Funds Appropriated Lighthouse Materials Sunk at Sea
1825	Lighthouse Built. In Service, December 17; however, Due to Notification Procedures, Light Turned Off.
1826	Lighthouse Re-lighted
1836	Lighthouse Burned by Seminoles
1837	Congress Approves Funds for Reconstruction
1846	Lighthouse Reconstruction Begins October 26
1847	Re-lit April 30
1855	Lighthouse Height Increased
1861	Lighthouse Sabotaged by Confederate Sympathizers
1867	Lighthouse Re-lit April 15
1875	Fowey Rocks Construction Begins
1878	Lighthouse Deactivated when Fowey Rocks Established Lens Shipped to New York (Staten Island Depot)
1967	Cape Florida State Park Opens in January
1968-70	Lighthouse Renovation
1971	Lighthouse Placed on National Register of Historic Places
1978	Lighthouse Reactivated (Lighted July 4th)
1990	Lighthouse Deactivated
1992	Hurricane Andrew
1996	Lighthouse Operational as Private Navigational Aid

HENRI-LEPAUTE, BUILDERS OF FRESNEL LENSES

With the exception of Alligator Reef, Henri-LePaute optic company of France constructed all the Fresnel lens for the Keys' reef lighthouses presently standing. Henri-LaPaute is one of several lighthouse lens manufacturers. Alligator Reef may not actually be an exception, because the identity of the person who built the lens has become lost information. Not only did Henri-LePaute build at least the majority of the lenses for the Keys lighthouses, its skilled craftsman built most of the Fresnel lenses used in Florida. Their lights shined forth along both of America's coastlines, in places like Cape Hatteras, and around the world, in places such as the infamous Devil's Island.

CAPE FLORIDA AND FOWEY ROCKS LIGHTHOUSES

Cape Florida Lighthouse failed to stop wrecks in the area. Thus, Fowey Rocks Lighthouse, a screwpile at sea, was built relatively close by. Fowey Rocks Lighthouse proved much more effective as an aid to navigation and thus Cape Florida Lighthouse was deactivated in 1878. It has been a private aid to navigation since 1996.

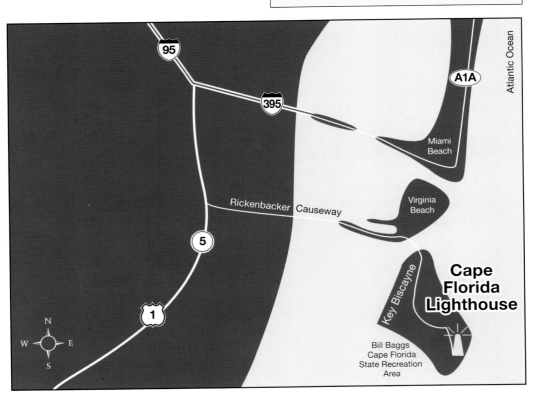

PC

CAPE ST. GEORGE
LIGHTHOUSE
(Franklin County)

On October 21, 2005, Cape St. George Lighthouse plunged into the sea. It happened on a day with big swells from Hurricane Wilma after many years of erosion. Local lighthouse enthusiasts are working to salvage the bricks to rebuild the lighthouse on higher ground, but this effort will take time if successful.

A string of four large barrier islands protects St. George Sound, Apalachicola Bay, and St. Vincent Sound from the full wrath of hurricanes and tropical storms. East to west these are Dog Island, St. George Island, St. Vincents Island, and St. Joseph Peninsula (no longer an island since silting sand has connected it to the mainland via a bayhead, which forms the enclosure of St. Joseph Bay). The barrier island of St. George stands guard offshore of the cities of Apalachicola and Eastpoint.

A causeway-and-bridge system connects St. George Island to the mainland from Eastpoint along US-98. At the east end lies St. George Island State Park, with beautiful beaches and hiking in a coastal scrub environment rich with wildflowers in season.

The Cape St. George Lighthouse can not be reached from the roads, however, or even by hiking west on the island beaches, for the lighthouse was separated because of a "cut" or channel dug through the island for navigational purposes. The Cape St. George Lighthouse stood on the far southwestern tip of the island, which is severed by this engineering feat. This portion of the severed island is referred to as Little St. George Island, and the dredged channel is known without affection as Government Cut or "Sikes' Cut," for the Congressman who promoted it. The cut is said by locals to have changed the direction of currents and diminished many land-side beaches in the area. It is possible it helped erode the sand from under the lighthouse itself.

The cut was very controversial locally. It was a project of powerful United States Representative Bob ("He-Coon") Sikes and saved Gulf boaters a little time by not having to go around St. George Island, the only known public benefit. Local boaters report that navigating the cut can be tricky, especially in storms or changing tides.

The lighthouse's former site can only be reached by boat. By the end of the 2004 hurricane season, the lighthouse was standing in the Gulf of Mexico before it fell. In the past, local guide services would take visitors to the lighthouse. These services have come and gone and come again, and it would be best to check with the Apalachicola Chamber of Commerce about guides.

Landing on the Gulf side of the island can be difficult, because there are at times, according to some area anglers, mighty, swift tides. The water around the docks is very shallow also. There is a landing, belonging to the Apalachicola Research Reserve, consisting of two docks on the bay side of the lighthouse. From the docks one must hike a little more than a mile to view the lighthouse's former site. Under the right conditions and in the right seasons, the hike is easy. In the hot summer months, it is a lot of work. It is also necessary to keep a lookout for occasional pygmy rattlesnakes and Florida cottonmouths (popularly called water moccasins), also plentiful on St. Vincents Island. During the warmer months, mosquitos can be fierce in the wilds on both islands.

Before it fell, the lighthouse teetered as much as 14 degrees off vertical. This tilt was corrected and the foundation replaced, but the erosion was extensive following the repairs. The light went out of service in 1994. Consequently, the Coast Guard closed

Top: Cape St. George Lighthouse before its fall (next page). It is obvious that the sea is encroaching on its foundation, giving a hint that the lighthouse will be in trouble if there is a big storm.

the station in 1999 because of safety concerns. The light was removed much earlier than 1999, however, probably in 1994. The Gulf, once 1,650 feet away, covers the lighthouse site at high tide.

The lighthouse was 74 feet tall with a focal plane of 72 feet. The builder was Edward Bowden. Originally, lighting was Lewis lamps, but a third-order Fresnel lens followed, built by Henri-LePaute, and yet another third-order lens made by L. Sautter (this last detail was revealed on a builders plaque uncovered when the lighthouse fell). The light has had three flash patterns: originally fixed white; in 1949, 10 second white flashes; and in 1977, a white flash every 6 seconds.

DIRECTIONS

The City of Apalachicola is located along US-98 to the east of Panama City. From US-98 in Eastpoint, turn south on G1A for the island, but not the lighthouse.

Those who wish to help raise the tower again can contact the St. George Light House Association (see Appendix A). Salvage and removal to the mainland was completed in 2006.

IMPORTANT DATES
1833 First Lighthouse Completed
1847 Second Lighthouse Built
1848 Second Lighthouse Lighted
1851 Second Lighthouse Destroyed by Hurricane
1852 Third Lighthouse Built
1857 Third-order Fresnel Installed
1861 Confederate Forces Remove Lens
1862 Apalachicola Taken by Union
1882 Fuel Changed to Mineral Oil
1899 Lens Replaced
1913 Incandescent Oil Vapor Lamp

1949 Lighthouse Automated
1977 St. George Island State Park Established
1999 Coast Guard Puts Light Out of Service
2004 Hurricanes Frances, Ivan, and Jeanne
2005 Hurricane Dennis
       October 21, Lighthouse Falls
2006 Lighthouse wreckage removed for later reassembly

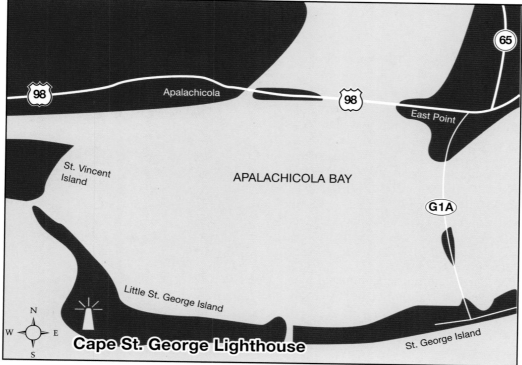

Top, left: An aerial view of Cape St. George Lighthouse after hurricane swells caused it to fall into the Gulf of Mexico in October of 2005. This lighthouse is being restored. The proposed new location for the tower is at the junction of G1A and the St. George Island Road.

Bottom, left: The dock at St. George Island.

Top: The hiking trail leading from the dock to the lighthouse.

A LIGHTHOUSE ROMANCE

It is possible to conjure a much more romantic feeling about Cape St. George than most lighthouses because of the romance of Pearl Porter and Herbert Marshall. Pearl Porter, the daughter of a long-time lighthouse keeper, Edward Porter, was courted by Franklin County Sheriff Herbert Marshall in the early 1900s. In order to woo her, Sheriff Marshall rowed a boat 6 miles from the mainland to the island and back, not once, but many times. This is a trip that by kayak can be grueling given the current, the distance, the sun in good weather, and the storms in bad. Some mornings, fogs are so thick one can't even find the enormous concrete-and-steel bridge between Eastpoint and Apalachicola. During some of the cooler mornings, the fog doesn't lift until afternoon.

Love conquered this gap, the tides, the currents, the fog, because Pearl married Herbert Marshall, and they had a long life together. The Porter House still stands, and it is on the Gulf side about 1 mile from the tower location.

CAPE SAN BLAS LIGHTHOUSE
(Gulf County)

A lighthouse was proposed in 1838 because of dangerous shoals reaching 4 to 5 miles from the Cape. However, a Captain Rousseau of the Revenue Cutter *Woodbury* reported the lighthouse would be a "useless expenditure." Captain Rousseau may have had in mind the weather and surf, for the first lighthouse built in 1847, despite Rousseau's cautions, only stood for four years, until a storm toppled it. The storm also took out the nearby St. Joseph Bay Lighthouse, by then already abandoned.

What the restless sea and powerful storms can do to the coastline of islands and lighthouses is clearly illustrated by lighthouses slightly to the west of Apalachicola and near Port St. Joe. Lighthouses at these locations have collapsed not once, but many times. It is true at Cape San Blas too. The coastline throughout the Panhandle is constantly attacked, washed away, and built up by the sea.

There have been four lighthouses at Cape San Blas, and the last one has been relocated. As previously stated, the first lighthouse, built in 1847, lasted a mere four years, coming down in an August 1851 hurricane. The second lighthouse went into service in November 1855 only to come tumbling down just ten months later.

To be colloquial, talk about having a hard time keeping a lighthouse operating! Perhaps Captain Rousseau, in his lifetime, felt justified in opposing a lighthouse at the Cape. The next lighthouse, built in 1859, was disabled during the Civil War and came down again in July 1882. It had stood 96 feet tall for 17 years, sending a revolving light visible 16 miles to sea every 90 seconds. That lighthouse also stood at times in the Gulf instead of on land because of storm-brought alterations in the islands.

In 1885, the current tower was built, but did not stay put. In 1918, the lighthouse, standing in the ocean, was moved again to its present location. This lighthouse was built in the north and almost lost when the ship bringing it sank. In the 1890s, the lighthouse was almost moved to Blacks Island. Those familiar with the area know Blacks Island as a substantial island in approximately the middle of the enclosed crook of St. Joseph Bay. This would not seem a very effective location for a lighthouse, and perhaps for that reason, the move was never made. Blacks Island, for years a place of primitive campers, was subdivided and put up for sale recently.

Almost the entire Gulf Coast is frequently shallow for some distance offshore. In portions of Northwest Florida, boats must risk the danger of running into rock on limestone shelves or beaching on sandbars. This shallow area often extends miles or more from land. Wrecks in the area have a long history, going back to early explorers. When Apalachicola was briefly the third-busiest port on the Gulf Coast during the time when cotton was king, navigational aids into the bay were badly needed, and included the Cape St. George Lighthouse and the lighthouses at Dog Island, which were later destroyed. Early shipwrecked travelers resorted to cannibalism in order to survive. A man and a woman survived the 1766 wreck of *The Tiger*, apparently by dining on a fellow sailor.

The first three lighthouses were built of brick, but the current operational, 96-foot structure is skeletal iron and is part of Eglin Air Force Base. It is a white, square, tower with an enclosed stairway. When operational, the light puts out 800,000 candlepower and flashes white every 20 seconds. The lens is a described as a third-order bivalve dating back to 1906. Third-order is a middle-power Fresnel, while bivalve essentially means it has two halves.

While the architect is unknown, the lighthouse builder was Phoenix Ironworks of Ocean City, New Jersey, and the lens was built by the French firm of Barbier, Benard et Turenne. The keeper's quarters were restored in 2005. They are affectionately known as "Sleeping Beauty."

DIRECTIONS

The turn to the lighthouse is not well marked, nor is the tower clearly visible from the road. The lighthouse is not open to the public. Despite reports in print that a museum and gift shop are planned, the lighthouse was fenced when lasted visited. Hope still abides for a lighthouse open to the public and a museum.

SR-30E, sometimes referred to incorrectly as a county road, is the main road out to the Cape and continues into St. Joseph Peninsula State Park after making a northerly bend. Long before it makes that bend, the lighthouse is on the south side.

From US-98, between Apalachicola and Port St. Joe, turn Gulfward on SR-30A and proceed to SR-30E. The lighthouse is at a public access to the beach long before the park and not marked as of the last visit.

The road to Cape San Blas dead-ends at St. Joseph Peninsula State Park, a wonderful place. Not only is camping possible, but there are fine cabins (reserve well in advance with the State Park) on what is arguably the finest stretch of beach in Florida and perhaps in the United States. The bayside of the island is rich in coastal scrub, and wildflowers in season are remarkable. There is no hunting in the state park, so animals, including deer, rarely bolt away, thus wildlife viewing is great too.

IMPORTANT DATES

1838	Lighthouse Proposed
1847	First Lighthouse Built
1851	First Lighthouse Destroyed by Hurricane ("...fell down during a gale in the autumn...")
1855	Second Lighthouse Built
1856	Second Lighthouse Destroyed by Storm Surge ("...the seas rose so high, they struck the keeper's door...")
1859	Third Lighthouse Completed
1865	Lighthouse Re-lighted After Civil War (July 23)
1882	Third Lighthouse Falls
1885	Fourth Lighthouse Built (June 30)
1918	Lighthouse Moved Due to Storm Erosion
1939	Radio Beacon Added
1996	Lighthouse Deactivated (January)
2005	Lighthouse Keeper's Quarters Restored

HOW A FRESNEL LENS REVOLVED

Three methods were used to make the Fresnel lens revolve. In the first and most colorful named of the three methods, the Fresnel lens rode around on "chariot wheels." These were usually brass, about 6 inches high, and worked like large ball bearings. While the chariot wheels were visible, ball bearings, another method used, were not. The third method involved a circular trough containing mercury on which the lens floated. Mercury is a hazardous material capable of causing death and serious disabilities. Its presence in the environment, whether in the tissues of fish or otherwise, is a cause of great concern. Because of this hazard, mercury floats have been replaced with ball-bearing systems.

A PLACE TO PRAISE

The Spanish had the right name for the Cape San Blas area. Accoding to Place Names of Florida, *the original name of the area was Cape San Plaise. The last Spanish word in that phrase means praise. Blas is likely an English-speaking corruption. Rich in natural beauty, the area is definitely praise worthy. St. Josephs Bay remains in pristine condition and can be experienced by boat or by driving along coastal roads. St Josephs Peninsula State Park has towering (for Florida) dunes and lonely stretches of seashore. The bay side of of the park has a lovely trail through coastal scrub.*

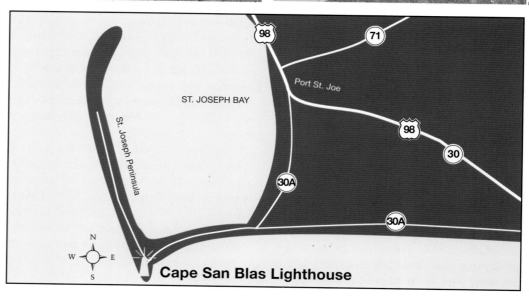

Cape San Blas Lighthouse

CARYSFORT REEF LIGHTHOUSE
(Monroe County)

Wreckers are salvors. That enormous living creature the coral barrier reef along the Keys lies in wait in all weathers for unwary ships. There is not a single lighthouse along the one hundred twenty miles of this monster from Carysfort Reef to Key West, and indeed, the influential wreckers of our town have vociferously opposed the setting out of any government lights. Some slanderers from the mainland have invented a story that Key West wreckers have actually set out a light at a place where there is no channel at all; the wreckers say to cynics who point toward a shining speck out there at night, No, no, that is just a star very low over the horizon.

John Hersey
Key West Tales

Carysfort is a dangerous reef with which many boats have collided. The results of such collisions has been lost cargo, grounded vessels, and loss of human life. Like Alligator Reef, Fowey Rocks, and American Shoal lighthouses, Carysfort was named after a shipwreck, in this case the October 1770 grounding of HMS *Carysford*. Some spellings make this Carriesfort.

Seventy-five years before the *Carysford*, HMS *Winchester* wrecked in the area. Almost two-and-a-half centuries later, in 1942, during World War II, the freighter *Benwood* was involved in a collision with another ship nearby.

It probably would have been more fitting if the reef had been named for the earliest wreck, but cartographers and chart makers had other ideas. The voyage and wreck of HMS *Winchester* cost many lives, some from the hurricane that dashed them onto the reef, others from an earlier sickness that swept the ship. The wreck was discovered on the reef in 1939, and subsequent research established that the ill-fated *Winchester* lost 342 men during its last cruise, all but eight of its 350-crew complement, a true nightmare at sea.

Before technology existed that allowed a lighthouse to be built at sea, in 1825 a lightship was floated briefly above the reef; it wrecked itself.

Carysfort Reef was not a screw pile. It was built with regular piles driven through disks. Sand Key was the first of the screw-pile lighthouses. With the screw-pile design, which was invented by Alexander Mitchell, an Englishman, it was easier to locate lighthouses on the reefs.

Standing 112 feet tall, the lighthouse greatly improved navigational safety within the area. The focal plane is an even 100 feet. The tower is a deep shade of red, made of iron, and octagonal in shape. It's skeletal design allows the wind to pass through.

The structure included a 3,500 gallon, freshwater tank. Thus the lighthouse held enough water to fill a moderate-size swimming pool. Most of the water was captured from rain gutters. Additional water was brought from Key West along with supplies by a tender vessel.

On its first day of operation, it was lighted by 18 Lewis lamps with 21-inch reflectors, and in 1858 a revolving, first-order Fresnel lens made its beacon visible for miles. The Fresnel lens is on exhibit at the Historical Museum of Southern Florida, located at 101 West Flagler Avenue, in Miami.

Currently, Carysfort operates with a modern Vega VRB-25 beacon which rotates and flashes white with red sectors. The lighthouse was designed by I. W. P. Lewis, and built by I. P. Morris and Company of Philadelphia, Pennsylvania, with Lieutenant George Meade as Chief Engineer, and received a first-order Fresnel lens made by Henri-LePaute.

LIGHTSHIP *CAESAR* AND THE DEATH OF CAPTAIN WALTON

Fifteen years before Carysfort Reef Lighthouse was operational, the Lightship Caesar *floated at Carysfort, warning of the reef. When the Seminoles burned the Cape Florida Lighthouse, killing one man and severely burning a keeper, the lightship became more vital.*

On June 26, 1837, Captain John Walton was the captain of the Lightship Caesar. *He brought with him his wife and children. A vegetable garden for the light station was kept on nearby Key Largo. Captain Walton and others set sail for Key Largo to gather some fresh greens. Captain Walton never made it back to the lightship or to his family. In a Seminole ambush, he was shot dead along with another sailor, and three wounded men escaped back to alert the others. Captain Walton is buried on Indian Key.*

DIRECTIONS

Carysfort sits to the east of Key Largo, from which Carysfort and Fowey Rocks lighthouses are visible.

THE DUELING LEWIS LIGHTHOUSE BUILDERS

Winslow Lewis, lighthouse builder and maker of patented Lewis lamps, bid to build a stone block lighthouse with a conical tower at Carysfort. His nephew, I. W. P. Lewis, another famous name in lighthouse construction, won the contract instead. A good part of the reason for this was that the younger Lewis in 1848 oversaw a study and consequent report on lighthouses. This study was critical in many respects of construction and upkeep. Since his uncle was the builder of many of these lighthouses, his efforts to fight back were to no avail. Carysfort is one of I. W. P. Lewis's lighthouses.

THE BLIND LIGHTHOUSE DESIGNER

The man responsible for the design of the screw-pile lighthouse lost most of his vision long before he made the design. Unable to read by the age of sixteen, nonetheless he went on to become a great engineer.

Alexander Mitchell, responsible for the "Mitchell Screw-pile Mooring," was born in Belfast, Ireland, in 1780 and died a few years before the American Civil War. He fled Belfast to Scotland during the Irish Rebellion of 1798, when he was all of eighteen years old.

He is responsible also for the Belfast Lighthouse on which he personally labored.

FROM CARYSFORT TO GETTYSBURG: GENERAL GEORGE MEADE

As a lieutenant, George Meade fought Seminoles twice in Florida, in the 1830s and 1850s, and he participated in the War in Mexico. He is best remembered for commanding the troops that defeated Robert E. Lee at Gettysburg through a defensive strategy. As a second lieutenant in the engineers, Meade designed, built, and/or worked on Cape Florida, Carysfort, Cedar Keys, Jupiter Inlet, Sand Key, and Sombrero Key lighthouses.

IMPORTANT DATES

1695 HMS *Winchester* Wrecked
1770 HMS *Carysfort* Wrecked
1825 Lightboat *Caesar* Stationed at Reef
1837 Captain Walton Killed
1852 Lighthouse Operational
1858 First-order Revolving Lens Installed
1913 Incandescent Vapor Oil Lamp Installed
1942 *Brentwood* Torpedoed
1960 Automated
1982 Vega VRB-25 Installed

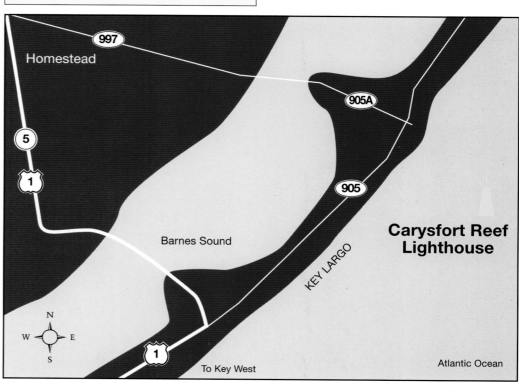

CEDAR KEYS LIGHTHOUSE
(Levy County)

The string of islands around the town of Cedar Key are largely in pristine condition. Oysters are abundant in the area, providing sharp shoals on which many inexperienced recreational boaters have stranded themselves for a tide or two. It is a wonderful place to wear polarizing sun glasses, for the waters are usually clear, and many fish can be seen.

During the last half of the 20th century, commercial fishing was a way of life, supporting perhaps a few hundred old-timers. With net bans to protect wildlife in the 1990s, commercial fishing slacked off and a new industry of clam farming arose. The area, however, was a seat of one form of industry or another for over 150 years. The shift from commercial fishing to clam farming was not the first industrial change in an area where sabal palm fiber was once made into building materials in a successor industry to cedar-tree harvesting.

Settlers began arriving on the two most prominent keys, Depot and Way, prior to the Civil War. The primary industry then was the harvesting of the plentiful cedar trees and the production of lumber. The products were shipped by sea, thus the need for a lighthouse. A railroad reached Cedar Key from Fernandina by the time the Civil War began.

During the Civil War, a Union naval blockade was broken by runners, who carried goods for the Confederacy. The lens disappeared into the Confederacy. What happened to it, no one is sure, although local reports are that it was buried.

Pencils of cedar wood were made at Cedar Key. Amazingly, more than 500 kinds of pencils were made by the pencil company. In present times, it is hard to imagine needing 500 kinds of pencils. However, those were the days when the closest thing to a computer was an abacus or the human mind, and a good pencil (and literacy) were prized possessions.

A hurricane in 1896 destroyed the cedar mill. It was a monster storm. It would likely have been classified a Category 5 storm if a classification system had been in use. Waves of 16 to 20 feet rolled over the islands. Boats were destroyed, an entire village wiped out. North and substantially inland at Lake City, on a path that should have greatly weakened the hurricane, sustained winds of 150 miles-per-hour were nonetheless recorded.

Cedar Keys also had the dubious distinction of being struck on September 20, 1950, by the first named hurricane. What a peculiar name - Hurricane Easy.

Hurricanes in those days were named for the phonetic, military alphabet. Easy struck the Keys first, ending a 28-year absence of cyclones, then hooked into the Gulf battering the coastline. It sure did not take it easy on Cedar Keys. It completely destroyed the local fishing fleet when it came ashore. It dropped almost 40 inches of recorded rain in two days at nearby Yankeetown, flooding rivers and streams and overfilling seasonal ponds. In Tampa Bay, the tide rose 6.5 feet above normal, flooding portions of the city that later became the home of the NFL's Buccaneers.

When the lighthouse was abandoned in 1915, it became a private residence. The owners added to the building. In 1936, Cedar Keys National Wildlife Refuge was created, and the lighthouse was included within the Refuge.

The lighthouse is located on Seahorse Key within Cedar Keys National Wildlife Refuge. Although it is on public land, access to the lighthouse is controlled, and one cannot just go there and see it. About a 20-minute boat ride from Cedar Key, the lighthouse has become a research station for the University of Florida where the Seahorse Key Marine Laboratory is located. From July 1 through April 30th, the beaches are open to the public, but the interior of the island is restricted year round in order to protect nesting seabirds. The lighthouse thus can only be viewed on a few days a year when an open house is held. The Refuge managers are the source for knowing when the open houses are being held.

The edges of the island support a population of Florida cottonmouths, popularly known as water moccasins. Naturalist Archie Carr wrote of gigging about a dozen in just a few minutes after arriving on the island. These robust, venomous snakes live beneath trees with nesting birds and are usually very dark in color with barely noticeable bands. They keep the raccoons from climbing up to eat bird eggs. On the other hand, the moccasins eat anything falling from the nests. A report appeared in print some years back saying there was a population of albino cottonmouths on the island. Not so, according to one wildlife officer, who says the snakes were not white but were perhaps covered with bird droppings.

There are perhaps a dozen great seafood restaurants in the town of Cedar Key. The town is laid-back, quaint, and has attracted its own share of peculiar and interesting characters. A band plays at the local hotel, a place something like the Eagles "Hotel California" to some. Other public lands nearby worthy of exploration include Lower Suwannee National Wildlife Refuge and Cedar Keys Scrub State Reserve. Cedar Key State Museum and Cedar Key Historical Museum are easily found in town. Both have valuable historical information on the lighthouse and the area.

As for the lighthouse itself, the 33-foot high tower is hexagonal, and the light focal plane is 75 feet. The tower sits atop the old dwelling which is very house-like and built of brick, iron, and wood. The original lens was a fourth-order Fresnel that cast a steady white light. The architect and builder were none other than Lieutenant George Meade, and the Fresnel was manufactured by Henri-LePaute. The light has not operated since 1915.

DIRECTIONS

Cedar Keys Lighthouse

JOHN MUIR PASSES THE CEDAR KEYS LIGHTHOUSE

John Muir, the great American naturalist and founder of the Sierra Club, once spent several pleasant and unpleasant months in the Cedar Keys. Muir, then not yet thirty, trekked alone from Indiana to the area, a journey described in A Thousand Mile Walk to the Gulf. Muir entered Cedar Key in October, 1867. He wrote he was able to smell the salt-sea for a day in advance; it reminded him of his native Dunbar, Scotland.

He describes a bustling port and a small village. Muir repaired a faulty wood planing device and was immediately offered work and lodging at a local sawmill, owned by a Mr. Hodgson. It was Muir's plan to earn a bit of cash in order to book passage on a ship to "the flowery plains or Texas" or to the West Indies. Unfortunately, he soon fell ill to a severe malarial fever, contracted in the swamps of either Georgia or Florida. So sudden was the onset that Muir fell unconscious several times on the short road between the village and the sawmill. He went unaided, mistaken as a delirious drunkard.

Mr. Hodgson took the ill Muir into the family home and gradually nursed him back to good health by constant infusions of lemons, limes, and quinine, plus rest. His convalescence lasted several months, and he then began walking explorations of the region.

One day, feeling somewhat stronger, he climbed the roof of the Hodgson home and sighted what he describes as "a pretty white moth" entering the harbor. This was the schooner Island Belle, on which he booked passage to Cuba, upon the next favorable wind. From Cuba, Muir made passage to New York, and thence, by way of South America, to California, where awaited the woods that were to become his passion and source of fame.

Contributed by Buck McMullen

Seahorse Key is the farthest west of the major named islands in the Cedar Keys area. It can only be approached by boat, and the lighthouse itself can only be visited on those few days when the interior of the island is open to the public. Reaching it requires a knowledge of the area or charts. To reach the town of Cedar Key, turn west from US-19 on SR-24 and follow it to the end.

IMPORTANT DATES

1854 Lighthouse Built (Lighted August 1, 1854)
1860 Cross State Railroad Reaches Cedar Key
1861 Confederate Soldiers Disable Lens
1862 Federal Forces Take Cedar Key
1866 Lighthouse Re-lighted
1869 Town of Cedar Key Incorporated
1896 Hurricane Destroys Cedar Mill
1915 Lighthouse Ceases Operation Building Becomes a Private Residence
1932 Trains to Cedar Key Cease Operating
1936 Cedar Keys National Wildlife Refuge Created
1950 Hurricane Easy Swamps Cedar Key
1953 University of Florida Marine Lab Located in Lighthouse

AS IT ONCE WAS

This black-and-white photograph from the private collection of Hibbard Casselberry shows Cedar Keys Lighthouse in a bygone era. Compare this to the photograph on the previous page and see what a difference a century or so makes. This is like having your own time machine.

Note that the original lighthouse was surrounded by a picket fence and lacked the two present wings. These wings were added during the time the lighthouse was a private residence. The original lighthouse is in a sandy, cleared area. The entire area has been grassed and trees have sprung up. From the modern-day photo, the casual observer would not realize that the lighthouse is located on an island. It likely helped in the brutally hot summers that there were windows and doors that could be opened on all four sides of the house. In current times, decorative fencing has been added to the block foundation.

Between the uniformed man at his leisure and the civilian in full coat, sits a small dog. Judging from the amount of clothing worn, this must have been a winter day, cloudlesss and cool enough for heavy clothing. A fine Florida day, but one that existed long before most of us were alive.

ISLAND HOTEL

Island Hotel in Cedar Key was built about 150 years before the publication of this book. Originally built as a general store on the cusp of the Civil War in 1859, it is a traditional part of a Cedar Key visit to stay in the hotel or enjoy the Neptune Bar.

According to history and legend, during the building's lifetime, it has served as a headquarters and billet for Union soldiers, a brothel, and a speakeasy. It is still possible to stay in one of the building's ten rooms by contacting the Island Hotel at 800-432-4640 or at www.islandhotel-cedarkey.com. Don't expect MTV, but the rates are reasonable.

Among the hotel's most notable guests was the author, Pearl Buck. While not all of Buck's books are set in China, she is best known for the epic novel The Good Earth and many other books set in China in the early 20th century.

Of the musicians reportedly in love with the locale, perhaps the one most known to those reading this book would be Jimmy Buffet.

Like the Stanley Hotel (Estes Park, Colorado) which allegedly inspired The Shining, the historic hotel in Cedar Key is said to be haunted. Thirteen ghosts were reported to dwell within its walls. Island Hotel is on the National Register of Historic Buildings.

CHARLOTTE HARBOR LIGHTHOUSE
(Charlotte County, Destroyed)

Like the Sanibel Lighthouse on nearby Sanibel Island, Charlotte Harbor Lighthouse was inspired by the cattle industry. The lighthouse at nearby Boca Grande was served in time by a railroad for the phosphate industry. The Peace River frontier was largely cattle country before phosphate deposits were found. There was a need to get the cattle to market, and there were two ways: long cattle drives or shipping the cattle to other foreign markets, such as nearby Cuba. The lighthouse was built to support these cattle shipments.

Built and lighted in 1890, the Charlotte Harbor Lighthouse was originally manned by a keeper and an assistant, but was unmanned by the end of World War I, and was in such a state of disintegration that, during World War II, it was torn down.

Charlotte Harbor Lighthouse had a focal plane of 40 feet, according to the website of the local Aids to Navigation Team. Its piles were iron, but it was built largely of wood, and looked like a house. It was lighted by a fifth-order Fresnel lens, which originally showed a fixed, red light, and later flashed white every 4 seconds. It was replaced by a simple lighted piling.

Charlotte County has had great concerns about the impact of phosphate mining on the Peace River and consequently on the rich estuary of Charlotte Harbor. The County has in recent years battled in court to stop the permitting of mines along the Peace River and especially Horse Creek. Florida's phosphate is used primarily in fertilizer and a large portion of it is sold to China.

COSGROVE SHOAL LIGHT
(Monroe County)

Despite the published reports of the Cosgrove Shoal Light demise, it is on the 2005 Coast Guard Light List. It is described as a hexagonal, pyramidal, skeleton tower on piles. The Coast Guard height is 54 feet, although other sources have given it an apparently incorrect height of 49 feet. The light has a range of 9 miles. The light flashes white every 6 seconds, and it was built in 1935. It is located 20 miles southwest of Key West.

AS SEEN APRIL 29, 1901

When photographed, this lighthouse was about a year old. Charlotte Harbor Lighthouse as pictured above is seen as it was more than 100 years ago on a day with sufficient wind that the flag is stretched out full mast. That flag did not have fifty stars, or even 48, as this was before the time Hawaii and Alaska became states instead of territories.

1901 was a turbulent year for the nation. For those alive in that time, there was plenty happening. In business, US Steel incorporated in New Jersey, thus becoming the first billion dollar corporation. J.P. Morgan created it, in defiance of anti-trust laws, in order to buy out Andrew Carnegie. US troops were still in occupation of Cuba, which passed a constitution similar to the American Constitution, and America held the Philippines, both outcomes of the Spanish American War. William McKinley was inaugurated as President and would be shot in September at the Pan-American Exhibition in Buffalo, New York; he died eight days later. The vice president, Theodore Roosevelt, who would say "Speak softly and carry a big stick," within a month of taking the office of President, invited Booker T. Washington to the White House. Roosevelt's invitation to a "person of color" infuriated many white people in the South. At the same time businessmen feared Roosevelt's populist attitudes and conservative bent.

CROOKED RIVER LIGHTHOUSE
(Franklin County)

Perhaps there should be a designation for the least-known lighthouse in Florida. Many people who regularly drive along US-98, have never seen nor heard of the Crooked River Lighthouse. Perhaps this is why one guidebook to Florida lighthouses does not include it. Nor is it included in the laminated *Pinpoint Guide to Florida Lighthouses*.

Much like the nearby Cape San Blas Lighthouse, it helps to have someone who knows where it is located. Asking at local gas stations isn't much help. "Lighthouse?" the attendant would likely say. "You must mean over at Little St. George Island, and it fell down."

One could stop at the alleged world's smallest police station in Carrabelle for directions. The city, like a lot of US-98, is quite different from Orlando or Miami. No building stands more than two stories and most folks know each other, except for those at the fancy new development up the road.

A few years ago, when lumbering activity was fierce at Tate's Hell State Forest, Florida black bears congregated around Carrabelle for reasons known only to black bears and were a nuisance with trash cans, not to mention dogs. In 2004, warning signs were placed along local highways slowing motorists to protect bears, which had returned again in goodly numbers. The main activities of the male citizens of Carrabelle, besides bear watching, seem to be fishing and hunting.

Tate's Hell? you ask. That sounds bad. According to folklore, a settler and hunter named Tate went in pursuit of his dogs, which, in turn, were after a panther. Lost for three days and bitten by a water moccasin, he stumbled out of the swamp, replying, when asked what happened, that he had been to Hell. There are also versions of this story where Tate arrives without his dogs and with them. In one version, Tate buried or lost his weapon in the swamp and offered a large reward for its return, a reward which no one could collect.

Built to support shipping for the lumber industry, the Crooked River Lighthouse takes its name from an inland river that joins the New River before emptying into the small estuary at Carrabelle. Lighthouses on Dog Island helped ships navigate dangerous waters, but the last one went down in a hurricane in 1873. Hurricanes in 2004 washed brick fragments from that lighthouse ashore.

Tides, currents, winds, and storms eat away and move around beaches in this area very vigorously. The Dog Island Light was replaced by the Crooked River Lighthouse in 1895, although it originally was intended to be placed on Dog Island. The general area is rough on lighthouses, as, for example, at Cape St. George and Cape San Blas. In fact, the Dog Island Lighthouse first operated in 1839 was itself rebuilt twice, in 1843 and 1852.

Dog Island is one of three barrier islands that enclose Apalachicola Bay. East Pass between Dog Island and St. George serves as an entrance to Apalachicola, as does West Pass between St. George and St. Vincent Island, and Government Cut, a canal through St. George Island. It was hoped that being on shore, Crooked River Lighthouse would not be so vulnerable to storms. Five people were swept to sea from the Dog Island Lighthouse during one storm.

The Coast Guard describes the Crooked River Lighthouse as made of iron, a skeletal cylinder, painted white, red, and black. Originally, the 103-foot lighthouse was lighted by a fourth-order Fresnel lens, later replaced by a 190-mm beacon which rotated. The focal plane is 115 feet, and there are 138 steps to the top. Every 12.5 seconds, a group of white flashes was sent from the lighthouse when it was operational. While the architect and builder are unknown, the Fresnel lens was manufacturer by Henri-LePaute in 1894. Crooked River Lighthouse is on the National Register of Historic Sites.

The original Fresnel lens is displayed at the Coast Guard District 8 Headquarters in New Orleans. The Carrabelle Lighthouse Association hopes for the eventual return of the lens.

There were two keepers' houses, one on either side of the lighthouse. In 1964, the homes were sold to individuals and moved from the site. One has since burned.

DIRECTIONS

Unlike Tate, today's adventurers can find the objective in only a few minutes, lose no dogs, suffer no venomous bites. After several trips back and forth through the small, attractive city of Carrabelle, and frantic searches in the *Atlas,* the lighthouse was found. The reason why it was so hard to find was evident. After it was built, pines had a chance to grow up and obscure it. Recently, some of the pines were removed, and it may now be easier to find. Crooked River Lighthouse is located slightly to the north of US-98, southwest of Carrabelle Beach. Its address is 1975 US-98 West. Another reference is that it is 2 miles west of the Tillie Miller Bridge in Carrabelle. A small sign announces it, but it could easily be missed in the blink of an eye. A dirt road leads up to it. The area around it is sandy, and one learns quickly it is filled with sand spurs, like many sandy parts of Florida.

A planned museum and gift shop had not materialized as of the last visit in 2006, although some of the land around it has been purchased by the city. Hope still blooms for the future of the lighthouse. Those who wish to help in the effort may wish to join the Carrabelle Lighthouse Association (address in Appendix A). Run-down and abandoned though it looked in its field of sand spurs, its skeletal design still had the noble appearance of a sentinel of the sea.

IMPORTANT DATES

1838-9	Dog Island Lighthouse Built
1843	Dog Island Lighthouse Rebuilt
1852	Dog Island Lighthouse Rebuilt Again
1873	Dog Island Lighthouse Destroyed
1875	First Lumber Mill in the Area
1893	Town of Carrabelle Incorporated
1889	Money Appropriated for Crooked River Lighthouse
1895	Lighthouse Built (Lighted October 28, 1895)
1933	Lighthouse Electrified
1964	Keepers' Houses Sold
1995	Lighthouse De-commissioned
1999	Carrabelle Lighthouse Association Formed
2001	City of Carrabelle Given Lighthouse for Preservation
2002	City of Carrabelle Allows Carrabelle Lighthouse Association to Manage the Lighthouse

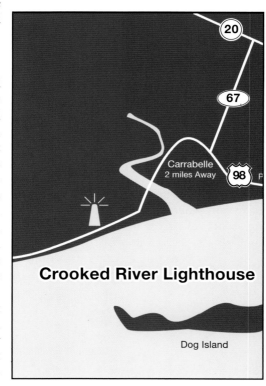

Crooked River Lighthouse

Dog Island

SS

DAMES POINT LIGHTHOUSE
(St. Johns County, Destroyed)

Very little is known of this lighthouse. As it was not at sea, but at a hard to navigate spot on the wider St. Johns, it required one of the less powerful Fresnel lens. It was either a fifth or sixth-order, putting forth a steady, white light. It was very house-like in appearance, perhaps similar to the house at Boca Grande, only much smaller. Contrary to published reports, no pilings remain. The former site of the lighthouse is directly under the A-9 Bridge over the St. Johns River. This tall structure is also designated Governor Napoleon Bonapart Broward Bridge. From I-95, exit east on A-9. A small park is located under the north side of the bridge for viewing the river.

IMPORTANT DATES
1857 Lightship Stationed
1872 Lighthouse Operational (July 15)
1893 Lighthouse Discontinued
1913 Structure Destroyed in Fire

DOG ISLAND LIGHTHOUSE
(Franklin County, Destroyed)

To illustrate how tough the Gulf and its storms are on beaches and lighthouses in the Florida Panhandle, one can look to Dog Island, where no lighthouse can be seen. Dog Island is to the east of Cape St. George Lighthouse and St. George Island.

A lighthouse was built in 1838 and helped guide ships into East Pass. Four years later, the October Hurricane of 1842 destroyed the quarters and damaged the tower. A repaired lighthouse was struck in 1851 by a storm that killed five people, who were washed away. The tower was replaced in 1852. Confederate troops carried off the Fresnel lens (fourth-order) during the Civil War, while Union forces apparently burned the buildings. In 1866, the light was re-lighted. Then, in 1872, the lighthouse tilted a foot off of plumb, and fell in 1873 during another powerful hurricane.

The architect, builder, and manufacturer of record was Winslow Lewis. There were 14 Lewis lamps with 16-inch reflectors in the first lighthouse. With the third lighthouse, a fourth-order Fresnel lens built by Henri-LePaute went into use in 1856; initially the light revolved and flashed white each minute. Dog Island Lighthouse was 44 feet tall with a focal plane of 48 feet.

DIRECTIONS
Dog Island is in the Gulf of Mexico, and the center of the island is south of Carrabelle. The island is parallel to US-98.

HOW LIGHTHOUSES GUIDE SHIPS

The U.S. Aids to Navigation System is designed for use with nautical charts. Nautical charts portray the physical features of the marine environment, including soundings and other submarine features, landmarks, and other aids necessary for the proper navigation of a vessel. This crucial information cannot be obtained from other sources, even ones such as topographic maps, aeronautical charts, or atlases. The exact meaning of an aid to navigation may not be clear to the mariner unless the appropriate chart is consulted, as the chart illustrates the relationship of the individual aid to navigation to channel limits, obstructions, hazards to navigation, and to the total Aids to Navigation System.

Sectors of colored glass are placed in the lanterns of some lights in order to produce a system of light sectors of different colors. In general, red sectors are used to mark shoals or to warn the mariner of other obstructions to navigation or of nearby land. Such lights provide approximate bearing information, since observers may note the change of color as they cross the boundary between sectors. These boundaries are indicated in the Light List and by dotted lines on charts. These bearings, as all bearings referring to lights, are given in true degrees from 000 to 359, as observed from a vessel toward the light.

Altering course on the changing sectors of a light or using the boundaries between light sectors to determine the bearing for any purpose is not recommended. The mariner must be guided instead by the correct compass bearing to the light and must not rely on being able to accurately observe the point at which the color changes. This is difficult to determine because the edges of a colored sector cannot be cut off sharply. On either side of the line of demarcation between white, red, or green sectors, there is always a small arc of uncertain color. Moreover, when haze or smoke are present in the intervening atmosphere, a white sector might have a reddish hue.

Lighthouses are placed on shore or on marine sites and most often do not show lateral markings. They assist the mariner in determining his position or safe course, or warn of obstructions or dangers to navigation. Lighthouses with no lateral significance usually exhibit a white light.

Occasionally, lighthouses use sectored lights to mark shoals or warn mariners of other dangers. Lights so equipped show one color from most directions and a different color or colors over definite arcs of the horizon as indicated on the appropriate nautical chart. These sectors provide approximate bearing information and the observer should note a change of color as the boundary between the sectors is crossed. Since sector bearings are not precise, they should be considered as a warning only, and used in conjunction with a nautical chart.

Ranges are non-lateral aids to navigation employing dual beacons which, when the structures appear to be in line, assist the mariner in maintaining a safe course. The appropriate nautical chart must be consulted when using ranges to determine whether the range marks the centerline of the navigable channel and also what section of the range may be safely traversed. Ranges display rectangular dayboards of various colors and are generally, but not always lighted. When lighted, ranges may display lights of any color.

Source: US Coast Guard

DAYMARKS

Markers with no lights are sometimes erected to assist mariners during daylight. Lighthouses are also each painted distinctively, especially when located near each other. This helps keep mariners from becoming confused.

IMPORTANT DATES
1838 Construction Begins
1839 Lighthouse Operational
1842 October Hurricane Damages Tower and Quarters
1851 Hurricane Damages Tower Five People Swept Away
1852 New Tower Built
1856 Fourth Order Fresnel Added
1866 Re-lighted After Civil War
1873 Hurricane Obliterates Lighthouse

FRENCH DOGS

Early French explorers named it Isles aux Chiens, the Isle of Dogs - Dog Island. No record exists to explain this unusual name. One theory is that wild dogs greeted the French, however it is possible they were wolves, for wolves were not then extirpated from the South. Two islands in the area are named from Spain (St. Vincent, a martyr) and England (St. George, the patron saint of England).

SEVERAL USES OF LIGHTHOUSES

Lighthouses that are not ranges can serve several functions:

1) they can mark a hazard such as a dangerous submerged rock (Carysfort Reef Light)

2) they can help mariners find the entrance to a harbor (St. John River Light)

3) they can serve as a landfall light (Hillsboro Inlet Light)

4) they can serve to aid a ship in determining its position at sea

5) sector lights. One lighthouse may fall into multiple categories. For example, Carysfort Reef Light serves the purposes of 1, 3, and 4.

1) To mark a danger, a lighthouse is sited on or next to the danger and ships know that as long as they stay away from the lighthouse, they're safe. This can be accomplished with a distinctive tower (during the day), or a distinctive light characteristic at night (or any light if the danger is some distance away from normal shipping routes). Several lighthouses in Florida have red sectors. Usually (but not always) the red sectors denote danger areas— a red light could indicate the ship is headed into an area of dangerous rocks.

2) To mark a harbor entrance, a mariner must properly identify the lighthouse either by its color and form during the day, or by its flash characteristic at night. Once the lighthouse is identified, the mariner takes a compass bearing and using that info, along with knowing where the lighthouse is in relation to the entrance, steers the proper course for the entrance. Here's an example. Amelia Island Light is south of the entrance to Cumberland Sound, which is an east-west channel. The mariner first identifies the lighthouse at night and it is directly to the west. He then should sail north until the lighthouse is to the southwest. He then would then need some other reference point (another lighthouse, a certain depth of water, a buoy ... just some other recognizable and charted reference point) before turning due west to enter the harbor.

3) If approaching Florida from the Bahamas, a mariner would want some hint that he was approaching the coast. While a sounding lead could be used to determine the water depth, a better way is to spot a lighthouse. A rough position can then be determined by noting the compass direction of the light, estimating the speed of the ship and then checking the compass bearing again after a known period of time. Another way of thinking about this use of lighthouses is the old call of "Land Ho!" when land is first sighted. At night, the the lighthouse will be spotted a long time before the land.

4) If two lights are visible at night, the mariner can take compass bearings to them and can then compute a very good approximate position by plotting the two "lines of position" on a chart.

Boxes on page 32 and 33 contributed by W. Williams.

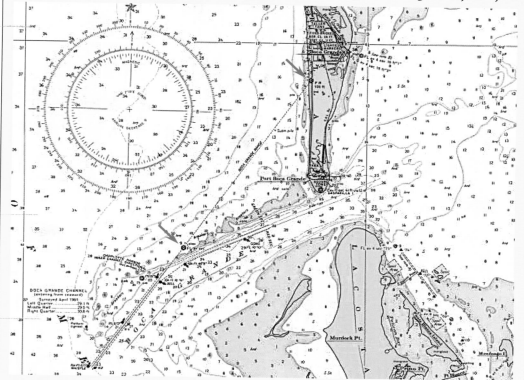

RANGE LIGHTS (ABOVE)

The two short red arrows on this nautical chart show the position of the two range lights at Boca Grande. The front range light is in the water, the rear range light is on the beach. By lining up the two lights, a ship's captain can position his vessel in the center of the approach channel (marked on the chart with a dotted line).

SOMBRERO KEY LIGHT (RIGHT)

Some of the red sectors used on lighthouses of the Florida Keys were established long ago, and their meaning is not clear to mariners. Sometimes there are explanations published in the "Coast Pilot", which is a reference book for mariners. One example of this is Sombrero Key Light. The red sector to the north of the lighthouse does not have a clear meaning. The red sectors to the east and west warn ships that they are approaching the reef and they should steer further south.

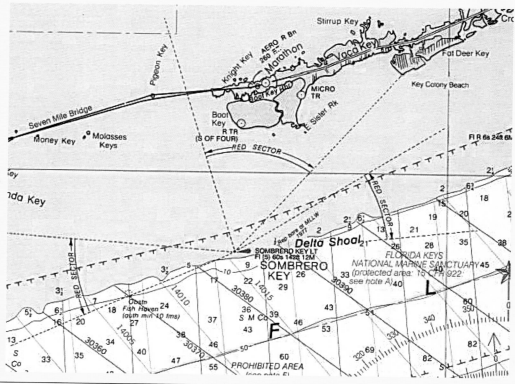

DRY TORTUGAS LIGHTHOUSES: TORTUGAS HARBOR LIGHTHOUSE
(Monroe County)

Garden Key's lighthouse, which is properly known as the Tortugas Harbor Lighthouse, is part of Fort Jefferson, an imposing, six-sided military fort in the Dry Tortugas, a small group of islands.

The islands are aptly named as "dry" because they have no freshwater source other than rare rains. According to *Gulf Coast Lighthouses,* Fort Jefferson was known as "Gibraltar of the Gulf." The Tortugas (turtles) are 69 miles west of Key West. The island chain was named by the Spanish for the plentiful sea turtles that abounded in the area. Marquesas Key lies about one third of the way from Key West to the Dry Tortugas. The Tortugas are reached by a half-hour seaplane flight or a longer boat ride from Key West. Despite their distance from land, the Tortugas receive quite a few visitors annually, up to 80,000.

Fort Jefferson was built with cisterns to collect rain water, the main one of which collapsed under the weight of some of the millions of bricks of which the fort is constructed. Some of the cisterns cracked because of poor foundations.

Garden Key is one of two lighthouses in the Dry Tortugas. The other is the Loggerhead Key Lighthouse, which is farther west. Separated by only 2.5 miles, they are closer together than any two lighthouses, except perhaps the two lights on Mayport Naval Station, unless you include rear-range lights, such at Boca Grande.

Fort Jefferson is the place where Doctor Samuel Mudd was incarcerated after the assassination of Abraham Lincoln by John Wilkes Booth. Booth leapt onto the stage at Ford's Theater, broke his leg, and Mudd set it when Booth was on the run. It is not clear that Dr. Mudd was aware of Booth's crime at the time he treated his leg. For this supposed crime, Mudd spent his time at Fort Jefferson on mundane cleaning tasks until yellow fever struck.

Doctor Mudd treated those stricken with yellow fever and is credited with saving lives. Mudd was pardoned after serving four years. In Mudd's time, more than 2,000 military men and prisoners inhabited the fort. Nowadays, at the right time, one can have the entire facility almost to oneself.

The fort was protected by 25-ton guns capable of firing a shell three miles. The guns were marvels of their time, thanks to Totten shutters, named after their inventor.

These shutters would rapidly open just after a cannonball was fired and close just as quickly once the ball was launched. This opening and closing was activated by gases from the firing of the weapon. The shutters were heavy steel. The short amount of time the shutters were open helped protect gun crews from potential enemy fire. The guns were never fired at enemies, however, as none ever appeared.

Fort Jefferson was never completed. By the time it reached the stage it is in today, boats could fire rounds that would crush everything - steel shutters, bricks and men.

In print, the number of bricks in Fort Jefferson has been estimated from 16 million to 40 million. It is often described as the largest brick fort or largest brick structure of its kind. Not having time to count the bricks, we shall just stand in awe at the notion.

In the 1800s, when vessels were primitively constructed and powered, tons of bricks were carted to the island, carried by prisoners and slaves, and mortared in place. It was an enterprise on a scale like that of the Egyptian pyramids.

The first lighthouse at Garden Key was constructed in 1826 and lighted on Independence Day, July 4th of the same year; this is very appropriate for a place named for Thomas Jefferson, one of the founding fathers of the United States, and principal author of The Declaration of Independence. This lighthouse was present long before Fort Jefferson was built.

In 1858, the lighthouse at Loggerhead Key (Dry Tortugas Lighthouse) was lighted. By the middle of the 1870s, the first Dry Tortugas Harbor Lighthouse was in disrepair and torn down as unsafe. It was replaced on April 5, 1876 by the current structure. A devastating fire in 1912, which was started accidentally by the lighthouse keeper, led to the automation of the lighthouse in 1913. In 1921, the lighthouse was deactivated. Maintenance is now in the hands of the National Park Service.

Like Fort Jefferson, the lighthouse tower currently standing has six sides. Twenty-five feet in height, it sits atop the brick structure of Fort Jefferson, which gives it a focal plane of 67 feet. It is referred to as the New Tower to distinguish if from the earlier lighthouse of which only the foundation remains. Within the tower, there are 33 steps.

The first lighthouse is referred to as the Old Tower. The Old Tower was lighted by 23 lamps with 14-inch reflectors. The New Tower, originally lighted by a fourth-order Fresnel lens, now shows forth from mere light bulbs, presenting a fixed white light. The architect and builder of the New Tower are unknown, but the Fresnel lens was built by Henri-LePaute.

IMPORTANT DATES

1825	Lighthouse Construction Begins
1826	July 4, Lighthouse Lighted
1847	Fort Jefferson Construction Begins
1856	Lighthouse Built on Loggerhead Key
1865	Doctor Mudd Imprisoned
1867	Mudd Treats Yellow Fever
1869	Mudd Pardoned
1874	Old Tower Deactivated
1876	New Tower Constructed
1910	Fort Jefferson Abandoned
1912	Fire
1913	Lighthouse Automated
1921	Lighthouse Deactivated

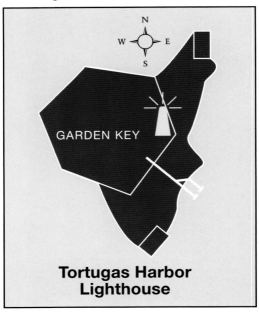

GARDEN KEY

Tortugas Harbor Lighthouse

REMEMBERING THE MAINE

From the earliest days of the United States, that collection of barely-more-than sandbars, called The Dry Tortugas Keys, were considered the means of controlling naval power in the Gulf, and for this reason the enormous brick edifice of Fort Jefferson was constructed. Of course, Fort Jefferson did not control the Gulf. The well located islands provided a sheltered and sufficiently deep anchorage to ships of war. These mobile gun forts, in turn, provided protection to the ports of Tampa, Pensacola, Mobile, New Orleans, and Galveston. As the age of wooden ships and sail gave way to steel-plated dreadnoughts fired by boilers, two coal-loading platforms were added to either end of Fort Jefferson. The battleship, USS Maine, whose explosion in Havana Harbor surely sparked the Spanish-American War, saw its last peaceful harbor while anchored in the shadows of Fort Jefferson, within sight of its parapet-mounted lighthouse, before steaming towards its fateful demise in nearby Cuba. Historians still debate the cause of the explosion.
- Contributed by Buck McMullen

Top left, above, and bottom: Views of Tortugas Harbor Lighthouse at Fort Jeffereson on Garden Key.
Top, right: A view from Dry Tortugas Lighthouse at Loggerhead Key.

DRY TORTUGAS LIGHTHOUSE
(Monroe County)

This lighthouse is popularly known as Loggerhead Key Lighthouse. Three lighthouses were built in the Dry Tortugas, two of which are still standing. In everyday conversation, folks refer to them collectively as the Dry Tortugas lighthouses and individually as the Garden Key and Loggerhead lighthouse. Those, however, are not official designations, and sometimes it can be confusing. There are also old salts and lighthouse buffs who talk about the New Tower and the Old Tower.

1. The first lighthouse in the Dry Tortugas was at Garden Key. That lighthouse is no longer in existence and is referred to as the "Old Tower" or Dry Tortugas Lighthouse.

2. The current lighthouse at Fort Jefferson on Garden Key is referred to as the "New Tower" or the Tortugas Harbor Lighthouse.

3. Dry Tortugas Lighthouse was the second lighthouse built in the Tortugas and is located at Loggerhead Key.

The Dry Tortugas Lighthouse was needed at Loggerhead because the Garden Key Lighthouse by itself was insufficient as an aid for mariners. Loggerhead is the largest key in the Tortugas.

Within the Dry Tortugas, Bush Key and Long Key are fairly substantial, and were confused by mariners of old, but the other named Keys shown on maps (East, Middle, and Hospital keys) are more microscopic, and many more shown on nautical charts smaller still. All these islands are located within Dry Tortugas National Park. Some of the Keys are entirely closed to visitors; some are closed during the nesting season of terns. It is best to check with the Park Service in advance, not only about access, but also about current conditions.

The Tortugas were named by Ponce de Leon during his explorations in 1513. The islands were named individually by an English cartographer. (A loggerhead is a type of sea turtle that nests in the area and along other islands and coastal Florida.) That map maker was George Gauld, and he mapped in the 1770s.

This lighthouse beacon shone for the first time on July 1, 1857 from the 157-foot tower (the focal plane is 151 feet). It was lighted by a second-order Fresnel lens. The lighthouse is modernized at present with a Vega VRB-25, a 12-volt rotating beacon with solar-powered batteries; it flashes white every 20 seconds. A conical, brick tower with 203 or 204 steps (there are different reports in print), the lighthouse is painted white half-way up, then black to the top. The architect is unknown, the builder Noah Humphries, and the Fresnel lens was made by Henri-LePaute.

Those who are interested in learning more about Loggerhead or Garden Key's lighthouses would do well to read Neil Hurley's excellent book, *Lighthouses of the Dry Tortugas* (see Appendix B), that explores their history and lore in-depth.

DIRECTIONS

Visiting Dry Tortugas National Park can provide a getaway from civilization and its conveniences. It is beautiful, if lonely there. For visitors without boats, there are tour boats and seaplanes available for charter from Key West. Some visitors bring kayaks and paddle in the natural splendor. Within the area are both reefs and shoals dangerous to ships traveling through the Northwest, Southeast, and Southwest Channels.

It is 2.5 miles from Garden Key and Fort Jefferson to Loggerhead.

IMPORTANT DATES

1825	"Old Tower" Built
1847	Fort Jefferson Construction Begins
1856	Loggerhead Lighthouse Construction Begins
1858	Lighthouse Lighted (July 1)
1873	"Old Tower" Deactivated
1873	Loggerhead Damaged by Hurricane
1876	"New Tower" Built
1910	Lighthouse Damaged by Hurricane
1931	Lighthouse Electrified
1945	Keeper's Dwelling Destroyed by Fire
1984	Fresnel Lens Removed
1992	Dry Tortugas National Park Incorporates Loggerhead and Garden Keys
1995	Vega Beacon Installed

Map, bottom: To see the position of the Tortugas Lighthouses in relation to Key West, refer to the map on page 3.

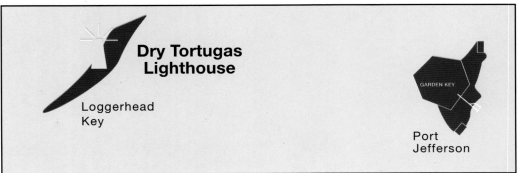

Dry Tortugas Lighthouse

Loggerhead Key

GARDEN KEY

Port Jefferson

36

BK

EAST WASHERWOMAN SHOAL LIGHT
(Monroe County)

The shoal and its light bear an intriguing common name. It has been suggested that perhaps the agitation of the small waves on the rocks looks similar to a washing motion. Another suggestion was that clothes from a shipwreck washed up close to or on it. There is also a West Washerwoman Shoal to the south of Sugar Loaf Key, named on a 1857 chart.

This unmanned, 36-foot light is located on the north side of the shoal, which is near Hawk Channel south of Boot Key, and flashes green every 4 seconds. The Coast Guard gives the visibility of the light as 5 miles. It is located on the left side of the channel when going north to south. It stands on a foundation that is black, triangular, and pyramidal.

Further information on East Washerman Shoal Light can be found in Neil Hurley's *Keepers* CD.

Right: An historic photo of the light.

EGMONT KEY LIGHTHOUSE
(Hillsborough County)

The visitor might spot a hunk of glittering metal sparkling in the sunlight at the water's edge of Egmont Key. It will not be a doubloon or pirate booty, but a spent brass cartridge - a treasure of another sort. The brass shell will be full of sand, not lead. It will be a "thirty-ought six," made and fired perhaps in 1918. Thirty indicates the caliber, and 1906 is the year the series started. It will be a rifle bullet fired by an American soldier during the First World War, almost certainly during rifle practice on Egmont Key. Imagine that. A lonely soldier - perhaps a long way from home, stuck out on a island, far from family and friends - fired that bullet, and by touching it, the visitor reconnects across time. Did he have a sweetheart at home? Did he need a pass to go into Tampa for a little weekend fun?

There are many reasons to hold Egmont dear besides such connections to history, including its vistas, lumbering gopher tortoises, attractive Florida box turtles, and its rich historical roots.

Egmont's scenic beauty is obvious. On the Gulf side is a pristine, isolated beach where one can walk accompanied by the the sound of the surf. No boom boxes, no jet skis, no one para-sailing. Along the gentle bay side, all that can be heard is the wind, while swimming fishes are revealed over the sandy bottom.

Like the sun, history lies rich on Egmont. If an historical quilt was sewed of every person and event whose mark was left on the Key over centuries, the images would represent the Spanish influence and the English, a lot of Americans, captive Seminoles, a monster hurricane, Civil War troops, and a lens made by a Frenchman, with Rough Riders passing by on their way to Cuba, and World War I soldiers.

Some historians believe that the first Spaniard to die in North America died here with Ponce de Leon's expedition for the Fountain of Youth. His must have been a forlorn death, so far from his native land, something like dying on Mars. The rugged lives of the Native Americans, whom Spain fought with, ruled over, and eventually extirpated, went unrecorded except through European eyes.

DeSoto certainly passed by Egmont on his voyages, a man who was capable, while leaving his wife in Cuba for safety, of letting his dogs loose on a Native American woman. A conquistador in search of treasures, DeSoto led an expedition that was large for its time, including horses and pigs and hundreds of men who kidnapped Native American guides.

Spain ruled Florida longer than the United States has been a country, and when it gave way to British rule, the Key was named for John Perceval, the Second Lord of Egmont, who is prominent in Amelia Island's history. The Egmont name stuck, while others vanished, perhaps because it now appeared on maps. British rule had little impact on Egmont Key, except to give it a name, nor did the new country of America impact Egmont much at first.

It wasn't until twelve years before the Civil War (in May, 1848) that a lighthouse was put on the Key. Then and now, Tampa Bay's entrance possessed many sandbars on which ships could become easily stranded. Now, of course, there is also the matter of the Sunshine Skyway Bridge and a shipping channel 40 feet deep. Even in the simpler 1840s, there was sufficient commerce and obstacles into and out of Tampa Bay that stranding became a problem.

The first Egmont lighthouse lasted less than six months. A hurricane washed over Egmont with waves 15 feet high. It was called the Great Hurricane of 1848, and it touched many Florida lighthouses with its fury. The Egmont lighthouse was badly damaged, but quickly restored and remained operational until the new lighthouse was constructed in 1858.

Imagine being that first lighthouse keeper! Talk about drama. He had his family with him. They survived the hurricane, but barely. The family tied the station boat to the top of a palm tree and huddled in the bottom throughout the storm. They must have prayed that rope held! They must have

experienced powerful churning seas, gale-force winds overhead, and torrential rains requiring frantic and constant bailing.

Before the second lighthouse was built, Seminoles forced to migrate to Oklahoma were relocated to Egmont Key. Among them was Billy Bowlegs, a chief who once was offered over $200,000 to move his tribe westward voluntarily. Perhaps he should have taken the offer, rather than making an attack in the Big Cypress which started the Third Seminole War. One can only imagine how Billy Bowlegs felt when forced onto the Trail of Tears.

The new lighthouse built in 1858 was outfitted with a Fresnel lens. At this time, it joined three other Gulf Coast lights, one at St. Marks, another in Key West, and the third at Cedar Keys, as remote sentinels on the West Coast. The new light is still operating, although it is no longer manned, as it was automated in 1990.

During the Civil War, Confederate troops abandoned Egmont to the Yankees. Before they did, not wanting to help the Blue Coats with navigation, according to Egmont Key State Park's brochure, they carried off the lighthouse's Fresnel lens.

The Union Army blockaded the Gulf Coast, and troops at Egmont were part of this effort. They went looking for the missing lens. Some historians say the taking of the Fresnel Lens sparked a Union Army invasion of Tampa, but the lens was long gone when the soldiers got there.

Perhaps it's time for Tampa to abandon Gasparilla, when the invasion of mythical pirate Jose Gaspar is celebrated, and instead hold Fresnelilla, when Blue Coats invade. Instead of tossing beads to young maidens enticed into popping open their blouses, as the pirates have for years, Union soldiers could reward the citizens who expressed willingness to return the lens.

Some historians report the lens was intentionally damaged by the Confederates so it could not be used, as happened to the Cape Florida Lighthouse and other lights the Rebels sabotaged as they abandoned them. This would make more sense, since the lens was heavy. Either way, the light was out of action during the Civil War, and Tampa will never replace Gasparilla with Fresnelilla.

The end of the War Between the States did not mean the end of soldiers coming to Egmont Key. During the Spanish-American War, Fort Dade was built to protect the citizens living in Tampa and about the rim of the bay. There probably was never much of a threat. Nonetheless, almost a half-million dollars was spent to establish the fort, in those days an enormous sum.

Along the west and north shores of Egmont are the fort's gun batteries, long silenced, some so well-preserved one can stand on them, others deteriorating and bearing signs that warn visitors to stay away. Two batteries on the southern tip are off limits to the public and slipping into the sea, due to erosion.

The batteries are named for soldiers who are now dust, and the artillery pieces are long departed. The gunners were sighting for Spanish ships of war, but as far as anyone knows, all they saw was water. A good tour of duty, as any soldier knows, is a boring one.

Down the middle of the Key runs a red-brick road that once connected barracks and military facilities, including a bowling alley, an early movie theater, a tennis court, and a gym. By 1906, there were some 70 buildings equipped with electricity and telephones.

Egmont was home to about 300 soldiers then. So many military men living on such a small island (1.5 miles long, .5 miles wide at the most) must have seemed a crowd. Daily formations surely took place each morning and evening on the brick, where military men stood at attention despite the buzzing mosquitoes and biting flies of summer. Taps and reveille were played, the American flag lowered and raised while men saluted.

In present times, on the south end of the Key is a building where harbor pilots stay. The Tampa Bay Pilots Association began operating from the island in 1926, three years after the fort was deactivated. The pilots are still there, guiding large vessels safely into Tampa Bay.

Currently, the most permanent residents on the island are reptiles and birds. Near the lighthouse, which is on the north end of the key, nearly tame gopher tortoises amble along while visitors enjoy their

Above, left: Unlike many other lighthouses in this book, Egmont's lighthouse has no enclosure for its beacon. Many of the modern optical devices are weatherproof.

Top, right: A bullet casing found on the beach, a thirty-ought six shell, probably fired in rifle practice when soldiers were stationed at the fort on the island.

Above: Old Egmont fortification. Soldiers were first stationed on Egmont during the Civil War.

Bottom, left: In the past, the old brick road on Egmont connected the barracks with other military facilities.

Bottom, right: Pristine beach on Egmont Key.

presence. Attractively-marked Florida box turtles are not as obvious, but are easily located by visitors walking the inland trails, which cannot be more than a mile long. Since Egmont is also a National Wildlife Refuge, all animals on it are legally protected and should be left alone and never fed.

Although there were reports that pygmy rattlesnakes were prolific on the island, none have been seen or found during many visits. While walking the trail and beaches, however, osprey and hawks can be seen swooping over the island. The ospreys catch fish, and the hawks try to steal the catch of the day.

The Key is currently co-managed by the State of Florida as a park and the National Fish and Wildlife Service, since Egmont is a National Wildlife Refuge, and its southern tip is off limits.

Egmont is also an historic site. No artifacts can be taken from it. Metal detectors are prohibited.

Originally built at 81 feet, the top of the lighthouse was removed in a cost-saving effort during World War II, which lowered it to its current 76 feet, with 99 steps from top to bottom. Some sources give the original structure a height of 85 feet. The current tower is brick, with an iron stairway, and cone shaped. While not open to the public, it can "walked right up to, and sat right down" beside. Originally lighted by a third-order, fixed Fresnel lens, currently a Carlisle and Finch DCB-24 Beacon rotates and sends out a white flash. A Tidelands 300mm Beacon is the current backup optic. Henry-LePaute was the manufacturer of the original Fresnel lens, and Augustus Angstrom the lighthouse builder. The architect is unknown.

Author's Note: The majority of the account for Egmont Key is a reprint of "Egmont Overture," an article originally printed in "Sarasota Magazine" in 2003, copyright Tim Ohr, with permission of the editor, Pam Daniel.

DIRECTIONS

If one drives over the Sunshine Skyway Bridge and looks to the west, Egmont Key is in sight. The Skyway was designated the Bob Graham Skyway in November 2005 in honor of a popular United States Senator.

Egmont Key is between Anna Maria Island in Manatee County and Fort DeSoto Park on Mullet Key in Pinellas County, yet perversely it is located in neither county. It is tenuously claimed by Hillsborough County, thanks to the magic of map makers.

While visitors to this State Park will have to pay for transportation or use their own boat to get there, at present there is no admission fee, since there is not a single place of entry to collect one. Activities permitted on Egmont include swimming, fishing, snorkeling, as well as touring the historical sites and wandering the trails. There are limited facilities (i.e., one composting toilet). Visitors should bring their own water.

One of the more interesting ways to reach the island may be by hovercraft. In the past, a hovercraft left daily from The Pier in St. Petersburg or from a location near Fort DeSoto Park. Other more conventional boats leave from the Pinellas County beaches. Currents are sometimes vigorous, swift, and dangerous.

IMPORTANT DATES

1837-8 Lighthouse First Suggested
1848   Lighthouse Lit (May)
1848   Lighthouse Damaged by Hurricane (September)
1858   Lighthouse Rebuilt
1861   Union Troops Occupy Egmont
1866   Re-lighted After Civil War
1926   Tampa Bay Harbor Pilots Begin Operating from Egmont
1944   Tower Rebuilt, Shortened, Electrified
1978   Egmont Placed on National Register of Historic Places
1990   Automated

THE NAME OF THE BEACON

What is a DCB Beacon? Mr. Garth Finch of Carlisle Finch, a beacon manufacturer, supplies this answer. "DCB means Directional Control Beacon. The model numbers of our beacons are either DCB24 or DCB224. You know now what the DCB stands for....and the 24 means 24 inches in diameter. The additional 2 means it is a double beacon, or two searchlight heads on the same motorized, revolving base."

VANISHING EGMONT

Egmont Key is suffering serious erosion problems. The palms in some of the photographs may have washed out to sea since their pictures were taken. The Key has been reduced almost by half its size from the 1800s. The Corps of Engineers has spent over a million dollars on feasibility studies about what to do concerning the erosion. In fact, some of the old military cannon positions are unsafe to walk on. Although one of the possibilities is to do nothing and let nature take its course, one hopes something will be done to preserve Egmont, if for no other reason, than because of its wonderful box turtles and gopher tortoises.

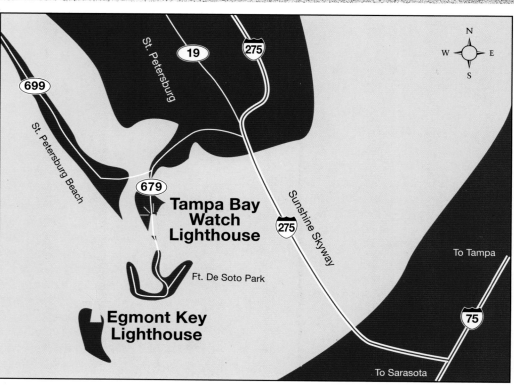

FOWEY ROCKS LIGHTHOUSE
(Monroe County)

The fifth, manned, screw-pile lighthouse built, Fowey Rocks Lighthouse, sits on a reef named for another lost vessel, in this case HMS *Fowey*, which smashed into the rocks in 1748, under the command of Captain Francis William Drake. This captain should not be confused with Sir Francis Drake, the English corsair, whose men raided Spanish St. Augustine in 1586, about 200 years earlier.

As if to emphasize the need to build the lighthouse, while it was under construction, two other boats shattered on the rocks. It is widely reported that the *Arakanapka* and *Carondelet* came close to striking the construction crew. (Latest research indicates that the name *Arakanapka* may be a corruption of *Arratoon Apcar*, a British Steamer sunk at Fowey in 1878.) The wreck of the *Arakanapka* (or *Arratoon Apcar*) grounded that ship irretrievably; however, the *Carondelet* was able to float away by tossing cargo overboard to the delight of many happy recipients.

Fowey Rocks, within the northern boundaries of Biscayne National Park, lies south of Bill Baggs Cape Florida State Park and 4 miles from Soldier Key, a very small island. Within the national park are the remains of over 50 wrecks, so many the National Park is creating an historical trail among some of them. This trail may in time extend to the entire Keys; like many things, it is a dream of humankind, and realizing it may take time. There are wrecks from all ages of going forth to sea in boats.

When Fowey Lighthouse was built, work crews lived on nearby Soldier Key and on a platform adjacent to the work site. Fowey was a successor light to Cape Florida Lighthouse, which the Lighthouse Board concluded in 1875 wasn't halting the wrecks.

On September 7, 1878, the newly-completed lighthouse was tested by a hurricane packing winds over 100 miles-per-hour. The timing of that hurricane was around Labor Day, when Florida has traditionally experienced some of its greatest devastation. The first hurricane was a shake-down for the lighthouse. More came, but none more powerful than Hurricane Andrew, providing the lighthouse with a Category 5 test in 1992. Andrew broke glass in the windows of the lantern room but left the structure still standing. Andrew was so severe, its name as a hurricane has been retired, and it will never be used again.

It's light cannot be mistaken for city lights, since it is located at sea, though in National Park literature Fowey Rocks Lighthouse has been nicknamed "The Eye of Miami." In the flatness of the watery landscape, the screw-pile lighthouses tower. On clear nights, it is impossible for approaching vessels to miss beacons coming from such height.

Built mainly of iron, Fowey has a tower 125 feet tall, with the light placed at a focal plane of 110 feet. The light is visible at least 20 miles away, flashing white every 10 seconds, with red sectors. The structure of Fowey Rocks Lighthouse is brown and the shape octagonal. The architect is unknown, the builder was Paulding and Kemble, Cold Springs, New York, and the Fresnel was manufactured by Henri-LePaute. For a brief period of time in the 1980s, Fowey was lighted by a flashing tube array, an experimental lighting method that was only tried for a short period of time.

DIRECTIONS
Fowey Rocks Lighthouse lies in the Atlantic Ocean within the northern portion of Biscayne National Park.

IMPORTANT DATES

1748	HMS *Fowey* Wrecked
1875	Lighthouse Board Approves Fowey Rocks to Replace Cape Florida Lighthouse
1876	First-order Lens for Fowey Shown at Centennial Exposition (Philadelphia)
1878	Lighthouse Built (Lighted September 7)
	Arraton Apacar Wrecked
1906	*Alicia* or *Alecia* Wrecked
1974	Lighthouse automated
1982	Modern Lighting, Flash Tube Array
1983	First-order Lens Sent to Coast Guard School (Yorktown, Virginia); Replaced with an Amerace 190-mm Rotating Beacon
1987	Modern Lighting Changed, RACON Beacon added
1992	Hurricane Andrew
1997	Vega VRB-25 In Use

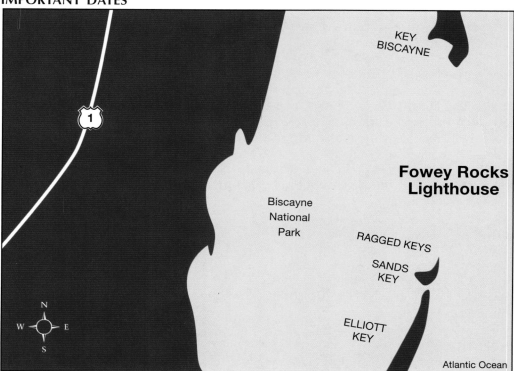

THE LIGHTHOUSE JUDGE
When a hurricane tested Fowey Rocks in 1878, on board was a young high-school graduate named Jefferson B. Browne who had become an assistant lighthouse keeper. Browne spent his time on the lighthouse studying law, and left a lighthouse-keeping career to attend law school at the University of Iowa, indeed a long and adventuresome throw in those days.

Ambitious and civil minded, he was elected attorney for Key West in 1880, fresh out of law school. Internet resources show a Jefferson B. Browne to have been elected President of the Florida Senate, to have been appointed Chairman of the Railroad Commission, and to have been a member of the State Supreme Court, from his election in 1916 to his resignation. He also found time to author a book, Key West: Old and New.

WRECKERS

The quickest route back to Europe from the Gulf of Mexico for many sailing boats was through the Straits of Florida. Shorter yes, but because they were so narrow and filled with shoals and reefs, this was a more dangerous course.

In times of Spanish, British, and United States governance, wrecking was a prime enterprise in the Keys. Unscrupulous men lured boats to wrecks with false lights, then profiting by salvage. However, plentiful wrecks occurred without this additional help, enough so that the prime business in the early Keys was salvage and repair.

In the beginning, salvage was largely unregulated, attracting Americans, Bahamians, Native Americans, and Spaniards from all points of the compass. It was sort of "get rich quick" through the misery of others; nonetheless, it was beneficial, like ants carrying away carrion, and at times captains of stranded boats struck deals with wreckers. Sometimes the extra manpower was helpful in lightening the load and freeing grounded vessels.

The business of wrecking eventually declined due to the construction of lighthouses.

SB

43

HEN AND CHICKENS SHOAL LIGHT
(Monroe County)

A number of unmanned, screw-pile foundation lighthouses were built, roughly in the 1930s, in the Keys in addition to those with quarters. Among these are: Cosgrove Shoal, Hen and Chickens Shoal, Molasses Reef, Pacific Reef, Pulaski Shoal, Smith Shoal, Tennessee Reef, Triumph Reef, and several more. Another may have existed in Biscayne Bay. This light, referred to locally as "a bug light," was seaward of Soldier Key.

These unmanned lights are rarely mentioned in print, perhaps because the human drama surrounding them is less well known as there were no keepers. All, however, are popular fishing or dive spots, and local boaters are familiar with them.

Hen and Chickens Shoal, a hazard to vessels using Hawk Channel, was the location of a Coast Guard buoy at least by 1919. Hen and Chickens Shoal Light is located south of Travenier and is 35 feet tall. It is within the Florida Keys National Marine Sanctuary. This light is still active, flashing red every 2.5 seconds.

The Florida Keys National Marine Sanctuary is one of 14 in the United States designated by Congress. Senator Bob Graham introduced legislation in 1990 creating the 2,800 square nautical mile sanctuary. The mission of the sanctuary is no less than to protect the coral reefs and marine environment. A number of private organizations and state and national agencies work with the sanctuary staff. More information is available on the sanctuary area at www.fknms.nos.noaa.gov.

The origin of the name of the shoal is an old mystery. It appears on a 1781 chart of the Florida Keys. The same name is also used for a shoal in New England and may have been adopted for Florida.

HILLSBORO INLET LIGHTHOUSE
(Broward County)

This lighthouse is also commonly referred to as the Hillsboro Beach Lighthouse. In everyday parlance, these names are interchangeable, but the official name is above.

Florida has many places named Hillsboro or Hillsborough, including the county in which Tampa is located and the river that supplies it with water. Actually there are places named Hillsborough up and down the east coast, even in New Jersey. According to Carmen McGarrry, Town Historian and President of the Hillsboro Lighthouse Preservation Society, there are more than 20 United States locations so named. How did this happen?

Blame a cartographer who wanted to please his boss, the Earl of Hillsborough, a man named Willis Hills, who was named Secretary of State for the Colonies in 1768, a few years before the American Revolution. In 1763, Hills was named President of the Board of Trade and Foreign Plantations. That year, Florida became a Crown colony. A map maker named DeBrahm was appointed Surveyor General of the Southern District, which included South Florida. DeBrahm placed the name Hillsboro on a map showing this inlet.

This lighthouse is a product of the 20th century. A group of little-known and unmanned lights in the Keys (for example Hen and Chickens Shoal) were built after it. Other "children of the 20th Century" include: the rear-range light at Boca Grande, built in 1927, and St. Johns River Light Station on Mayport, built in 1954.

In 1907, Hillsboro Inlet Lighthouse went into service after four centuries of wrecks on area reefs by European and American vessels. In World War II, German submarines, the Wolfpack, hunted off Florida's Atlantic Coast, and, in 1943, one sub was reported sunk in the area. Earlier, in 1942, a tanker was sunk offshore.

According to the Coast Guard, the height of the Hillsboro Inlet Lighthouse from mean high tide to the focal plane is 136 feet. There are differing heights in print. The light emits white flashes.

Currently, there are two deluxe keeper's cottages and a one-bedroom cottage that senior Coast Guard officers use for their R&Rs. In addition, there is a garage/storage building and a former radio building used as a mini-museum. A hurricane in 1926 caused a breakwater to be built, which was completed in 1930.

The top half of the lighthouse is painted black, the bottom half white. This is its daymark. Black is seen better above the treeline, while white is seen better against the trees.

The flashes are sent through a remarkable Fresnel lens. The individual sections or panes of the lens are curved, triangle-shaped glass. The lens operated flawlessly for 85 years. A broken gear brought the flashes to a halt in 1992. A rotating beacon then replaced the Fresnel lens. The Fresnel lens support was later re-designed and re-installed in 1999. The original lens' support had a mercury float that was hazardous. The floating system and motors were replaced by a modern ball-bearing system in 1999 and 2000.

Hillsboro Inlet Lighthouse is an attractive, octagonal, skeletal iron, two-tone lighthouse. It is lighted with a second-order bi-valve, which casts light perhaps 20 or more miles to sea. Planes approaching the metropolitan area can pick up the light from a greater distance because they are not hindered by the curvature of the earth.

For five years beginning in 1992, Hillsboro Inlet Lighthouse was lighted by a 190-mm beacon which rotated, and for

HILLSBORO INLET SPEAK-EASY

During the great social experiment called Prohibition, the teetotalers tried to force the drinkers to go dry; alcohol was made illegal. "Speak-easys" were illegal bars where one spoke the password quietly at the door to gain entrance. According to The Florida Lighthouse Trail, *a book sponsored by the Florida Lighthouse Association, the brother of the lighthouse keeper provided illegal rum at Club Unique. Among the guests were allegedly President Roosevelt and Prime Minister Churchill on hush-hush, war-time business. The two leaders, however, were never there at the same time. The* Florida Lighthouse Trail *from Pineapple Press is a must for the lighthouse enthusiast.*

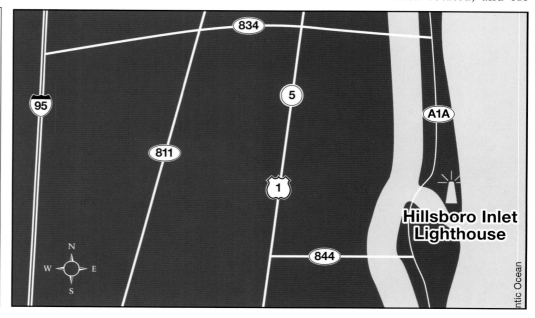

Hillsboro Inlet Lighthouse

three years, beginning 1997, it was lighted by a VRB 25 Beacon. The reinstalled Fresnel lens flashes white every 20 seconds. The tower has 175 steps.

The lighthouse architect was the Office of Lighthouse Engineers (Charleston, South Carolina), the builders Russell Wheel and Foundry of Detroit, Michigan and J. H. Gardner of New Orleans, Louisiana, and the lens was built by Barbier, Benard, et Turenne, Paris, France.

DIRECTIONS

The lighthouse is located on Hillsboro Inlet along A1A, north of Pompano Beach. This area, west of the Intracoastal Waterway, is locally known as the City of Lighthouse Point, and during the last decade or two, the light itself is sometimes called "the Big Diamond," because of the diamond-shaped glass panels of the lantern room. This lighthouse is not open to the public, except one day every quarter of the year via the preservation society, but there is an excellent website (see appendix), museum and gift shop.

IMPORTANT DATES

1851 Lighthouse First Proposed
1886 Lighthouse Proposed to Congress
1903 Lighthouse Funded
1904 Land Purchased
1905 Further Funding
1906 Construction Begins
1907 Lighthouse Completed in March
1911 School With Nine Children Established at Lighthouse
1913 Schooner *Alice Holbrook* Ran Aground
1925 Electricity Lighted the Tower East Keeper's Quarters Moved to Hillsboro Club
1926 Hurricane Damages Lighthouse Property, Wood Bridge Built at Inlet
1930 Breakwater Created
1942 Tanker *Lubrofol* Torpedoed Nearby
1943 German U-Boat Sunk
1947 Hurricane Damages Keeper's Cottages
1978 Placed on National Register of Historic Places
1997 Hillsboro Lighthouse Preservation Society Formed
1998 Vega VRB-25 Optic Installed
1999 Flotation System for Fresnel Reinstalled (Lasted One Month)
2000 Commercial Type Ball-Bearing System Installed
2002 Barefoot Mailman Statue Moved to Station
2003 Dedication of 37-Cent Stamp "Hillsboro Inlet, Florida"
2005 Hurricane Wilma Downs Many Trees and Damages Cottage Facade
2006 Centennial Celebrations (March 2006 to March 2007)

JUPITER INLET LIGHTHOUSE
(Palm Beach County)

Some people wrongly believed the town of Jupiter and its Inlet got that name because of the space program. Jupiter and Canaveral are on the same coast separated by perhaps less than 100 miles. In fact, the name is quite old and predates the arrival of the Europeans. Native Americans called this area *Jobe*, the source of Hobe Sound. English cartographers decided *Jobe* looked a lot like Jove, thus in time it became Jupiter or Jove, the main god of the pagan Roman pantheon. The lighthouse deserves such a name, for it is a very impressive and beautiful structure.

A Fort Jupiter was manned in the area during the Second Seminole War in the 1830s and was abandoned in 1858. The location of Fort Jupiter was 2 miles upstream from the lighthouse. While the light would have helped guide supplies to Fort Jupiter, the primary reason for building the lighthouse was as an aid to coastal navigation. Work was stopped for fear of attacks during the Third Seminole War.

Designed by then Lieutenant George Meade, this conical-shaped, red-brick lighthouse with its delicate top of glass is certainly one of the more attractive of Florida's lights. Some would argue it is the most attractive. The tower is adorned with a light room above a lattice and portholes.

Meade was transferred to the Great Lakes District in 1856 before the construction began. The man who brought the lighthouse materials on a tender in 1859 was Edward A. Yorke, about whom little else is known. He served as a hands-on construction supervisor.

$35,000 was appropriated in 1853 and the site selected in 1854, but construction took six years, much longer than planned. Reportedly, 50 trips were necessary to haul the construction materials 35 miles from a staging area at Fort Pierce to the north. The trip from Fort Pierce was made by way of the Indian River, a long, bay-like enclosure of saltwater protected by islands to the east. Such a lengthy trip in such primitive times may well have resulted in a trip of a day or even longer, with an overnight encampment at the construction site, and a return the next morning. The Indian River, while enclosed from the sea, is still capable of substantial waves and whitecaps under stormy weather conditions, thus, as with all the Florida lighthouses, construction was not easy.

The lighthouse went into service in July 1860 on the eve of the Civil War. Construction, already slowed by the shifting sands and the Third Seminole War, was followed very shortly by the light becoming nonoperational, as rebel partisans disabled the Fresnel lens so that the light could not function through its very first year. Some well documented accounts say that the lens was carted off, even though this was a first-order lens requiring a lot of carting.

Such a difficult and trying start, however, was followed by years of continuous service. During the war, Captain James Armour helped guide Union soldiers who retrieved the Fresnel lens or its parts, put the light back into service, and served for the next 42 years as lighthouse keeper. Armour was one of a small group of "volunteers" who helped the Union Navy capture Confederate blockade runners heading from Jupiter and the Indian River Inlet to Nassau.

Near the lighthouse now is the Loxahatchee River Historical Society, a museum, and a gift shop. The Jupiter Inlet Lighthouse is said to be the oldest standing structure in the county.

The 108-foot lighthouse (also given in print at 105 feet) has 105 steps (also given in print as 112) and a focal plane of 146 feet (also given in print at 150 feet). The Coast Guard height from mean high tide to the focal plane is 147 feet. Thanks to elevation, and with a first-order Fresnel lens, it may be seen perhaps 20 miles or more away at sea by low riding boats. Aircraft and taller boats will see it even sooner. The elevation is thanks to Native Americans who created a shell mound on which the lighthouse stands.

Originally the lens flashed white at 90 second intervals. The current beacon is more complicated, with two 1 second flashes every 30 seconds. The first first-order Fresnel lens was built by L. Sautter and Company and replaced with a Fresnel lens built by Henri-LePaute. The architect was Lieutenant George Meade, and LePaute's Fresnel lens continues to shine from the lighthouse in modern times.

The keeper's quarters were built to hold three families. They burned to the ground in 1927. The oil storage house still stands. This account was greatly improved thanks to the kind assistance of James D. Snyder, who has a recently published book, *A Light in the Wilderness: The Story of Jupiter Inlet Lighthouse & the Southeast Florida Frontier*. Mr. Snyder assures us that the lighthouse has 105 steps. As docent on Saturdays, he has heard many children count out the steps from bottom to top and vice versa.

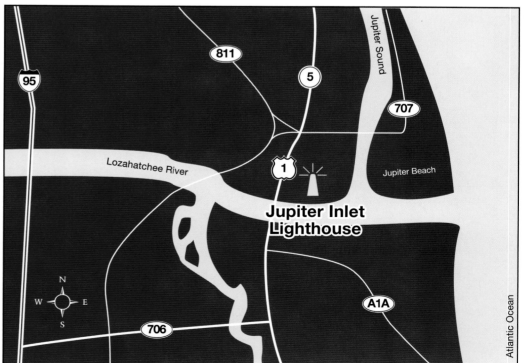

SS

DIRECTIONS

From I-95, go east on Indiantown Road approximately 6 miles to US-1. In Jupiter, go north approximately 2 miles on US-1. The lighthouse is on the northeast bank of the Loxahatchee River. The lighthouse is located in Lighthouse Park. The excellent museum and gift shop are located a mile from the lighthouse and are not open daily. It would be best to contact them (see Appendix A) for current operating hours.

Jonathan Dickinson State Park is nearby and a worthy historical visit. After a shipwreck in 1696, Dickinson and his family were captured by Native Americans. Jonathan Dickinson's journal, in which he recorded his harrowing experiences, has been reprinted and is available at the park. The State Park is remarkable also for its fine, scrub-adorned hiking trails and the state-designated canoe trail on the Loxahatchee River.

IMPORTANT DATES

1838 Army Post, Fort Jupiter Reservation, Established
1853 Congress Authorizes Lighthouse
1854 Lighthouse Site Selected
1860 Lighthouse Lighted (July 10)
1861 Lens Disabled or Taken By Confederate Sympathizers
1866 Lighthouse Re-lighted
1866 Kerosene Replaces Lard Oil
1898 Telegraph Added
1905 Naval Radio Station Added
1911 Telegraph Station Built
1927 Original Keepers' Quarters Burned
1928 Lighthouse Electrified Lens Damaged in Hurricane
1973 Placed on National Register of Historic Places
1987 Lighthouse Automated
1994 Loxahatchee River Historical Society Begins Offering Public Tours
2000 Two-year Restoration Completed

Opposite page, and top: The photo on the opposite page shows the Jupiter Inlet Lighthouse with the moon rising. Compare the color of the tower in this photo with the photo at the top of this page. The top photo shows the lighthouse tower with a fire engine red color. After restoration in 1991, the color of the tower was returned to the more natural brick red color shown on the opposite page. This towering lighthouse serves as a navigational beacon and helps guide vessels to the inlet.

KEY WEST LIGHTHOUSE
(Monroe County)

When Ponce de Leon sailed to the Keys in 1521, he named them "The Martyrs." Viewed from a distance, he thought they looked like suffering human beings. In those days, the islands were not connected and were remote, lacked water, and were mosquito plagued. Someone living on them would have had a rugged life.

"The Martyrs" is hardly the image today of the Keys and particularly not of Key West, aptly named as the westernmost of the Keys connected by the Overseas Highway. The town was historically a maritime and military center after the Native Americans were dispersed. Today, Key West has a reputation for being laid-back, a fun place for tourists, famous for Key-lime pie, and the home of artists, and authors.

It was almost 400 years between Spanish exploration and Flagler's railroad, which reached Key West in 1912. The completion of this railroad was the end of a Florida, railroad-building saga which began in 1883, when Henry Flagler, a partner with John D. Rockefeller in Standard Oil, purchased the 36-mile Jacksonville-St. Augustine-Halifax Railroad and drove it south to Miami and eventually Key West. Portions of the railroad path can still be seen, such as a ramp of the old railroad bridge at Bahia Honda State Park, among the few remaining pristine public beaches on the way to Key West.

The Overseas Highway, or US-1, followed the railroad's path to Key West, arriving in 1938, while jumping from island to island over bridges built by the railroad, some short, others long, like Seven Mile Bridge (actually about 6.75 miles). Measured in Mile Markers, US-1 dead-ends in Key West, the end of a trek for millions of tourists.

Flagler's railroad, often declared the Eighth Wonder of the World, was washed out of existence by the Labor Day Hurricane of 1935, but the Overseas Highway still stands on the original railroad bed, which is constantly repaired, and sometimes jammed with traffic. For much of its length, it is highly scenic, with water vistas on both sides of the highway.

In the hurricane which destroyed the railroad, over 400 people died, including rescue workers traveling Flagler's railroad, who died when their train was overwhelmed by the sea. Overseas Highway and its bridges are sometimes damaged by storms. Hurricane evacuations of the Keys are frequent between June and October.

Powerful hurricanes arrive in Key West only impeded by barrier reefs, or fortunately for the Keys, slowed by the massive island of Cuba with its mountains, to the south.

When people say Cuba is 90 miles from Florida and the United States, they mean 90 miles from Key West.

In October 1846, a massive tidal surge, fostered by a hurricane, smote the first Key West Lighthouse killing fourteen. The lighthouse was destroyed and the keeper's family devastated. That lighthouse went into service on March 10, 1826 and lasted 20 years. The first Key West Light was lighted by 15 lamps and 15-inch reflectors. It was located on Whitehead Point, where its foundation remains.

In modern times, Overseas Highway, radar, and weather forecasting have made it possible for citizens to live on the Keys and evacuate before massive storms arrive; many chose not to. Prior to Doppler radar, weather satellites, and automobiles, however, there was (for a long period) just a blow, giving little warning when the storm was coming, or where the storm was going. At the turn of the 20th century, telegraph lines between Cuba and Key West gave some warning if the storm passed over Cuba.

The rebuilt lighthouse went into operation in 1847, was made of brick, initially 60 feet tall with 20 feet added in 1894. While the initial focal plane was 67 feet, the current focal plane is 91 feet above sea level, thanks to slight elevation. The rebuilt light was cast by 13 oil Lewis lamps with 21-inch reflectors. A third-order Fresnel lens was installed in 1858. The lights put forth a fixed white light. Built of brick and iron in typical conical shape, the tower is white, and there is a black, iron housing for the lantern. The architect was Smith, Keeney, and Holliday, the builder was Duncan Cameron, and the Fresnel lens by Henri-LePuate.

Several lighthouses were built on reefs around Key West. These lighthouses helped shipping and thus industry and growth. The most significant of these lighthouses, however, were the Key West, Northwest Passage, and Sand Key lighthouses.

IMPORTANT DATES

1822 Key West Purchased for $2,000 from Juan Pablo Salas
1825 First Lighthouse Built
1826 Michael Mabrity First Keeper
1832 Mabrity Dies, Succeeded by His Wife
1836 "Old Ironsides," the USS *Constitution*, Visited Key West
1846 Lighthouse Destroyed, Mabrity Children Killed
1846-7 Second Lighthouse Built
1847 Lighthouse Lighted
1858 Third-order Fresnel Installed
1873 New Lantern Installed
1886-7 Original Keeper's Quarters Replaced

THE LADY LIGHTHOUSE KEEPER
Whe the first keeper of the Key West Lighthouse died of yellow fever in 1832, his wife became the official lighthouse keeper, a duty she performed alone for 32 years, then performed with an assistant up to the Civil War. In 1846, an horrific hurricane that predates meteorological record-keeping, swept over Cuba and descended on the Keys. Many lighthouses become places of shelter during storms. This has happened on Sanibel Island in the past, and it happened at Sand Key and Key West during this hurricane, in both cases with tragic results. The lighthouse, smacked by hurricane-propelled, giant waves, fell and killed the lighthouse keeper's children, but not Barbara Mabrity, who somehow survived the toppling. Nothing remained but the foundation, and that wasn't found until modern times. When the new lighthouse was built, Mrs. Mabrity was named keeper.

1894-5 Lighthouse Height Increased (Also given incorrectly as 1892)
1912 Flagler's Railroad Reaches Key West
1915 Lighthouse Automated
1927 Lighthouse Electrified
1935 Labor Day Hurricane Severs Railroad
1969 Lighthouse De-activated
1972 Leased to Key West Art and Historical Society
      Becomes Private Aid to Navigation
1989 Lighthouse Restored and Opened to the Public
1990 Keeper's Quarters Remodeled
1998 Nominated to National Register of Historic Places

HOW KEY WEST GREW

At the start of the Civil War, Key West had less than 3,000 inhabitants, yet was considered Florida's largest city. After the Civil War, the town was home to a large cigar industry, which later moved to Tampa. This industry's growth was spurred by Cuban refugees and avoidance of import taxes. In the 1880s, Key West was still Florida's largest city, with under 10,000 folks. In the 1930s, Federal projects kept Key West afloat, as it was a city with an 80% unemployment rate. In addition to its connection to the Overseas Highway in 1938, Key West's growth was spurred in 1940, during World War II, when water pipes were run from the Everglades. The population quickly went up by 300%, reaching 45,000. Then came air-conditioning, and the population soared!

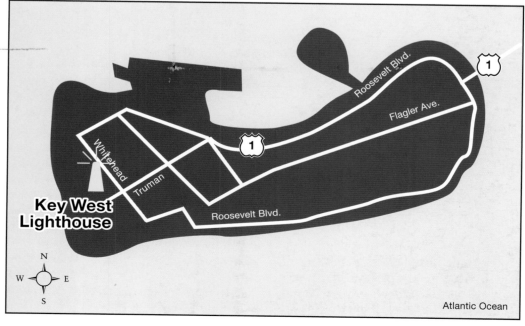

DIRECTIONS

Take the Overseas Highway (Route 1) to Whitehead Street. The lighthouse location is obvious. An excellent museum with gift shop is open to the public and just across the street is Hemingway's home. Hemingway penned many of his best-known novels there. *To Have and Have Not*, set in Key West, is the story of Harry Morgan, a floundering charter-boat captain, who turns to smuggling. The book contrasts the lives of the rich and the poor.

Opposite page: A view from the top of Key West Lighthouse.

Above, left: A first-order Fresnel lens on display at the lighthouse museum.

Above, right: The Key West Lighthouse.

MOLASSES REEF LIGHT
(Monroe County)

The 45-foot light (from mean high water to focal plane) was erected in 1921. This light is relatively little known and designed to be unmanned. It utilizes screw-piles and is built in a pyramidal, hexagonal, and skeletal design.

Molasses Reef Light was located within John Pennekampf Coral Reef State Park. The seaward boundaries of the State Park were redrawn sometime in the 1970s or 1980s so that they extended only 3 miles into the sea. The lighthouse is 4.5 miles offshore. Molasses Reef is now within Florida Keys National Marine Sanctuary.

The light is south of Key Largo.

MULLET KEY LIGHT
(Hillsborough County)

Mullet Key lies at the outer mouth of Tampa Bay. The water to the south of the Key lies in Hillsborough County, while the Key itself belongs to Pinellas County. In fact, the water off the Key forms a jagged demarcation between the two counties.

It is a guess that this lighthouse was located in what is Hillsborough County based on the fact that the photograph provided by Hibbard Casselberry shows the light standing in the water.

A 38-foot high, black structure on piles, little is known of Mullet Key Light, which is now vanished. It was active with a lamplighter in 1912, with a fixed white light.

Apparently, Tampa Bay had several other lighthouses in the early 1900s, which have also vanished. One of them was at the Hillsborough River and was attractive enough to be pictured on a postcard of the times.

Neil Hurley reports that the shoal was chartered but not marked in 1855. A 36-foot structure on Mullet Key was documented as late as 1959. In 1997 and

2000, a unlighted marker sat on the Key. Neil Hurley believes a daybeacon may still mark the shoal, although it is not found on the current Light List.

NINE-FOOT SHOAL LIGHT
(Monroe County)

In 1911-12, one person was assigned to maintain this light, which is the earliest indication of when it was operational. This person, however, was more like a lamplighter than a keeper, for he didn't live at the light. This light is active on Hawk Channel near East Washerwoman Shoal, and built on a teepee-like design of tied piles known as a dolphin. It flashes white every 2.5 seconds and is apparently 18 feet tall. It marks one of the entrances into Marathon's Boot Key Harbor.

NORTHWEST PASSAGE LIGHTHOUSE
(Monroe County, Destroyed)

The name breathes romance - *The Northwest Passage.* Yet there is little known about the lighthouse located there, and some of that is unclear.

The passage was a shortcut between the Atlantic and the Gulf of Mexico. It saved mariners of smaller ships from having to go around Rebecca Shoals, quite a considerable distance. The depth of water in the channel did not allow deep-draft ships to make use of it.

Before there was a lighthouse, there was a lightship, the *Key West.* It was located near shoals approximately seven miles northwest of Key West. The lightship successfully weathered hurricanes and repairs for more than a decade but was not cost effective. The lighthouse and its keepers also had hardships to experience. A lightship tour of duty was probably no fun. There would be worries about other ships running into the lightship, plus the problem of seasickness in stormy seas.

Delayed by yellow fever and storms, the lighthouse was built in 1855. It had its share of damage and repairs, including an earlier fire and myriad hurricanes and wood rot, and was deactivated in 1921, 50 years before another fire finished off the wooden house. Ruins can still be viewed. Charts should be consulted or, better yet, a charter boat used.

The Northwest Passage Lighthouse was a screw-pile built of iron and wood. It was lighted at first by a fifth-order Fresnel lens, which gave off a steady, non-revolving white light. The characteristics of the light were changed several times.

The lighthouse was not affected by the

Civil War and was in service during the war years.

Although a screw-pile, it was not skeletal in appearance, but very house-like, and must have been a pleasure to be aboard during good weather. It was reported to have been pilots quarters and even one of Hemingway's homes (it was not). Surely boaters climbed aboard, fished from it, and slept in it, before it was abandoned. Now only its pilings remain.

Although assembled in Philadelphia, apparently the builder is unknown, as is the architect. The fifth-order Fresnel lens was built by L. Sautter.

An extensive account about this lighthouse appears in Love Dean's superior book *Lighthouses of the Florida Keys.* Neil Hurley has written an account that appears in *Florida Lighthouse Trail.*

Top, left: Northwest Passage Lighthouse

Top, right: Pacific Reef Lighthouse

PACIFIC REEF LIGHT
(Monroe County)

Pacific Reef Light is a skeletal, pyramidal, hexagonal, iron, screw-pile, designed to operate unmanned. It may be named for the vessel *Pacific* that wrecked on East Key in the Dry Tortugas in 1857.

Built in 1921, the height from mean high water to focal plane is 45 feet. This tower is at sea, located 3 miles southeast of Elliot

Key and within Biscayne National Park, as are Fowey Rocks Lighthouse and the Boca Chita private building of a lighthouse design.

The lantern room was removed from Pacific Reef Light. It is presently a monument in Founders Park in Islamorada.

Contrary to reports, this is an active light, and it can be seen for 9 miles.

PELICAN SHOAL LIGHT
(Monroe County)

Pelican Shoal Light was pointed out to the author by Hibbard Casselberry, past president of the preservation society for Hillsboro Inlet. According to Neil Hurley, "Pelican Shoal is not mentioned in the 1920 Coast Pilot." The first entry is in the Coast Guard Light List from 1955. "That entry says that Pelican Shoal was established in 1939 and rebuilt in 1951."

Currently an active light, it is located in 16 feet of water, stands 36 feet, and is a red light that flashes every 6 seconds. The house structure probably was intended originally to hold acetylene tanks to fuel the light. Acetylene came into use during World War I and continued into the 1950s and 60s, when battery power replaced it.

The light sits atop a structure referred to as a dolphin. This is a foundation of several piles tied together at the top like a teepee.

A small light, but visible for 7 miles, Pelican Shoal is just south of American Shoal.

PENSACOLA LIGHTHOUSE
(Escambia County)

On board Pensacola Naval Air Station, this lighthouse sits in a beautiful, coastal-scrub habitat. On sandy, coastal trails, military men and women workout, taking jogs beneath sand pines. Not far away is the bustling city of Pensacola, the western edge of Florida, which would touch Alabama, if not for the Perdido (Spanish for lost) River. To the east lies Santa Rosa Island, while to the west is Perdido Island. Between these two islands lies the entrance into Pensacola and Escambia bays, hence the location of the Pensacola Lighthouse.

The Naval Air Station was smacked hard by Hurricane Ivan in 2004 and Dennis in 2005. Today the Naval Air Station is home to the Blue Angels, the famous, formation-flying jet fighters. As in many hurricanes past, devastation in 2004-5 was monstrous in places because of erosion. There was substantial damage also to Pensacola Naval Air Station. The Naval Air Station lies within Gulf Islands National Seashore and has many historic sites, including an unforgettable military cemetery, a fort, and the lighthouse.

The oldest city in Florida is St. Augustine, which is also the oldest continually-inhabited city in the United States. Pensacola is Florida's second-oldest city and was a city under both Spanish and British rule. When the state was ruled by Britain, Pensacola was briefly the capital of West Florida. The importance of Pensacola as a port was immediately evident to colonial powers; it was contested and fought over by France, Spain, and England.

No one is quite sure what the words Escambia (for the bay and county) or Pensacola (for the bay and city) mean, but there are various, conflicting theories. There is no doubt of some Native American origin, perhaps mingled with Spanish, but of which tribe, no one is sure.

President John Adams commissioned the naval base during the infancy of the nation. The original light was built of brick and iron in 1824, when the naval base was established. The current light went into operation in 1858. The new lighthouse was needed not because the old one was destroyed or non-functional, but because the sands shifted, changing the location of the channel. The first lighthouse was a mere 30 feet tall plus a 7-foot lantern, yet because of elevation had a focal plane of 80 feet. It was lighted with Lewis lamps plus reflectors, and put forth a white flash every 35 seconds.

Two rear-range lights were used with the new lighthouse starting in 1859. The Fort Barrancas Rear-Range Light was discontinued 71 years later. By the time of the Civil War, there were at least five lights in use (two ranges front, two ranges rear, and Pensacola Light). At one time, the lighthouse itself served as a rear-range light.

Other rear-range lights were located at Fort McRee on the bay's west entrance. The Fort McRee Lights, also lighted in 1859, had a focal plane of 56 feet and were lighted with a lantern. During the Civil War, the lights were destroyed and not replaced until 1888. In 1918, the lights were automated but destroyed in a storm in the 1930s.

The present lighthouse possesses the highest focal plane in Florida at 191 feet from a 150-foot structure. It is cone-shaped and made of brick, with a black lantern, and has 177 steps. The first lighthouse was lighted with Lewis lamps. The second lighthouse had a first-order Fresnel lens, taken or disabled by Confederate forces in 1861. After the war, a first-order Fresnel lens was installed. The light put out a white burst every 20 seconds.

At present, the top two-thirds of the lighthouse is black, the bottom third white. The architect of the first tower was Winslow Lewis and the builder Benjamin Beall. Captain John Newton, United States Army, was the builder of the second tower. The architect of the second tower is unknown, but it was lighted with a revolving, first-order Fresnel built by Henri-LePaute.

It should be noted that the books in print disagree about many of these points, including such basic things as the height of the lighthouse itself.

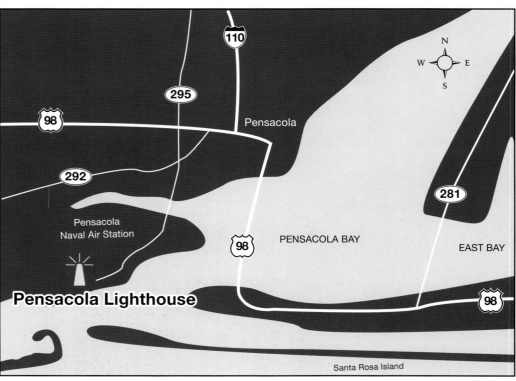

IMPORTANT DATES

1823 Lightship Located in Pensacola Bay

1824 Original Lighthouse Built
Lighthouse Lighted (December 20)

1854 New Lighthouse Funds Appropriated

1856 Construction Begun

1859 Lighthouse Lighted (January 1)

1859 Rear-Range Light Added

1861 Confederate Forces Hold Lighthouse
Lens Removed

1862 Confederates Leave Area
Union Forces Install Temporary Lens

1879 Renovation of Lighthouse

1888 Rear-Range Light Relocated

1930 Rear-Range Lights Discontinued

1938 Lighthouse Electrified

1965 Lighthouse Automated

DIRECTIONS

From I-10 above Pensacola, take SR-291 south. Turn west on US-98, and shortly go southwest on SR-292. Turn south on Duncan Road, and cross a short bridge to the military police guarded gates. The MPs can provide directions if maps are unavailable.

With all visits, it is best to check in advance. Currently, the schedule is for the lighthouse to be open to the public on Sundays from the first Sunday in May until October 30th, but that could change. Of course, the lighthouse can always be viewed from outside, unless for some reason the base is not open to the public.

Opposite page: One room at the museum display.

Left: A view of the Fresnel lens at Pensacola Lighthouse Museum.

Top, right: The lighthouse sits in a coastal scrub habitat.

PONCE DE LEON INLET LIGHTHOUSE
(Volusia County)

Besides a gorgeous appearance, Ponce de Leon Inlet Light Station has many interesting points associated with it. It has history, tragedy, mystery, literary reference, and is the tallest lighthouse in Florida.

The inlet giving the lighthouse its name honors Juan Ponce de Leon, the Spanish explorer. It is he who named the state *La Florida,* the land of the flowers, during his alleged search for The Fountain of Youth. Historians are often not certain which places Ponce de Leon, DeSoto, and other Spanish explorers landed and visited, and this is true for the Inlet bearing Ponce de Leon's name.

For a while, most of Florida was a county called Mosquito County. This was in territorial times. From Mosquito County was carved two counties, St. Lucie and Escambia, before statehood. New Smyrna was first county seat of Mosquito County and then of St. Lucie County.

Ponce de Leon Inlet was known as Mosquito Inlet, not the sort of thing the chamber of commerce would like to use to promote an area. Long ago, Mosquito was a pretty appropriate name for many Florida places, as those of us know well if we moved to Florida or were born here before massive clearing and the application of mega-tons of malathion. The name was changed from Mosquito Inlet in 1927 to Ponce, or Ponce de Leon Inlet, but before then, the official designation was the Mosquito Inlet Light Station.

The red bricks of this structure shine in the sun and shimmer in the summer heat. The appearance is definitely "lighthouse," substantial, and rock solid. Some consider it Florida's premier lighthouse.

A National Historic Landmark, the tower is constructed of over a million bricks, with impressive walls 8 feet thick at the base, and a foundation sunk 12 feet into the earth. That's a lot of bricks and a massive foundation. Speaking of foundations, it should be noted that the architect for the lighthouse, Frances Hopkinson Smith, owned the company which built the base for the Statue of Liberty.

After North Carolina's Cape Hatteras, Ponce de Leon Inlet Light Station is the second-tallest lighthouse in the US, and one of the most visited. The present lighthouse, completed in 1887, was the second intended here for the inlet. (The 1835 lighthouse was located on the south side of the inlet, while the current lighthouse is on the north.) The lighthouse focal plane is 159 feet according to the Coast Guard Light List.

When you look at this magnificent structure, it is hard not to be glad that the first lighthouse built at Mosquito Inlet was never lighted. According to *Bansemer's Book of Florida Lighthouses,* this was because fuel was never supplied to light the lamps. According to De Wire's *Guide to Florida Lighthouses,* no light fixture was sent. The Light Station reports a lighting system from Winslow Lewis was sent. When no oil arrived, the keeper stored the reflectors in a trunk in his house. In October 1835, a seven-day storm swept the house and reflectors away. The reflectors may have washed back to shore since one was found by a settler and another appeared in the possession of Coacoochee, a Seminole leader.

This first lighthouse (built in 1834) was also kept from activation because of the Seminole strife. The structure was damaged by the 1835 storm, and eventually toppled in 1836, allowing the present lighthouse to be built.

There are treacherous waters offshore. *The Florida Lighthouse Trail,* published by Pineapple Press, reports that in 1565, an entire French fleet wrecked during a hurricane, with at least 70 reported wrecks in the centuries following. Hundreds of wrecks have probably occurred in the area in recorded maritime history.

Building the current lighthouse was not an easy task, and human lives were lost in the process. De Wire puts the count at seven, while *The Florida Lighthouse Trail* reports that in 1884 four drowned, including the chief engineer (Orville Babcock) during a spill while rowing between their ship and the construction site. The manager of the Light Station writes: "Over a dozen people died during the construction of the Light Station."

Working the lighthouse was no easy task either. Fuel for the lantern was hand-carried up 213 steps to the lantern room - potentially deadly in Florida hot summers.

An original, first-order, fixed Fresnel lens was installed in 1887. This lens was believed lost. The lens was latter found, reappearing in 1998 inside the Seaport Museum at Mystic, Connecticut. The lens was returned to Ponce Inlet and is on display in the Lens Exhibit Building.

Light from the tower produced a beacon that reached perhaps 20 miles out to sea. In 1933, the original light was replaced with a third-order, rotating Fresnel lens. Deactivated in March 1970, the lighthouse was reactivated in 1983, almost one hundred years after it was built. When the lighthouse was shut down in 1970, the tower fell prey to vandals.

In 1972, the town of Ponce Inlet was deeded the Light Station, the Ponce de Leon Inlet Lighthouse Preservation Association was formed, and restored it as a museum. The museum remained after the lighthouse was reactivated. In 1996, a modern device, a Vega VRB-25 Beacon, was installed. Initially the light emitted six flashes every 30 seconds. The modern pattern is white every 10 seconds.

In 2004, the third-order, rotating Fresnel lens was reconstructed from its individual glass pieces and replaced the Vega beacon. This good work was funded through Volusia County and the Ponce de Leon Lighthouse Preservation Association. The current characteristic is six 0.5 second flashes in 15 seconds, followed by a 15-second eclipse. The beacon is now a private aid to navigation.

The architect of the tower was Francis Hopkinson Smith, the first-order, fixed Fresnel lens was built by Barbier et Fenestre and the third-order, rotating Fresnel lens by Barbier, Bernard, et Turenne.

There were a number of builders. Talk about personnel turnover! The following chronology was offered by the museum. Chief Engineer Orville Babcock drowned in the inlet in 1884. George D. Benjamin, Babock's choice as Superintendent of Construction, was removed and replaced in 1885. Jared A. Smith was Chief Engineer after Babcock. Chief Engineer James F. Greogry replaced Smith in 1886, and was in turn replaced by J. C. Mallery in 1887. Superintendent H. Bamber in July 1885 created a special "working platform" scaffold to build the tower. Foreman of Works William L. Smith started in November 1885 but died the following March. He was replaced by William Strachan. George A. Rains was appointed to replace Mr. Strachan, but the appointment was canceled by the Secretary of the Treasury, who asked Frank M. Jolley to accept the position. Jolley declined, and William Mickler was hired only to be fired by Gregory one month later. Gregory himself was then fired as Chief Engineer and replaced by J. C. Mallery.

Opposite, top: Ponce de Leon Lighthouse was built after many wrecks had occurred in the area over a period of time. It is an impressive structure with supporting buildings and keeper's quarters.

Opposite, bottom: A dizzying view of the spiraling staircase within Ponce de Leon Lighthouse.

IMPORTANT DATES

1569 Spanish Explorers Name the Area Mosquito Inlet
1834 Funds Appropriated
1835 First Lighthouse Built
1835 First Lighthouse Destroyed
1882 Funds Appropriated
1887 Second Lighthouse Lit (November 1)
1897 Stephen Crane Rowed to Safety
1909 Incandescent Oil Vapor Lamp Installed
1926 Renaming of the Inlet and Lighthouse
1952 Lighthouse Automated
1970 Lighthouse Shut Down
1972 Deeded to Town of Ponce Inlet
1972 Lighthouse Listed on National Register of Historic Places
1996 Vega VRB-25 Beacon
1998 Secretary of Interior Declares Lighthouse a National Historic Landmark
2004 Third-order, Rotating Fresnel Lens Returned to Service in the Tower.

DIRECTIONS

At the eastern dead-end of I-4, exit onto I-95 south. Take exit 256, Dunlawton Avenue, east to South Atlantic Avenue. Go south 5 miles to the lighthouse.

There is both a museum and a gift shop and excellent displays at the lighthouse. In 2005, a living history program called "Climb with the Keepers" began. This tour, which has a special fee, takes 90 minutes and raises funds for preservation of the lighthouse.

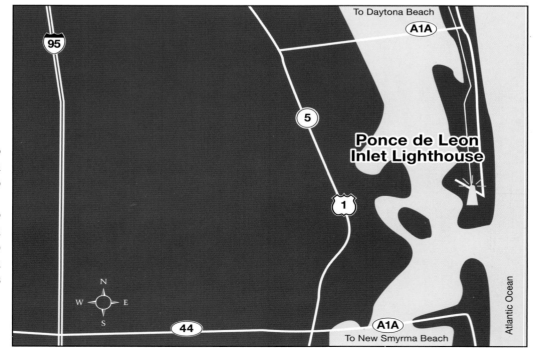

Above: The shadow of the tower as seen from atop Ponce de Leon Inlet Lighthouse.

STEPHEN CRANE: THE RED BADGE OF COURAGE

Stephen Crane, is the author of The Red Badge of Courage, a famous novel of the Civil War published in 1895. The novel concerns bravery, cowardice, honor, and at times has been mandatory reading for high-school students. This classic of a young man encountering the violence of war was written at the time by a man who never served in the military, yet it is startling in its realism.

Crane was a journalist who wrote two books of poetry and six novels, only two of which are easy to find now; the other, Maggie: A Girl of the Streets, is about a New York prostitute. His short stories are widely anthologized.

Crane was forced to abandon the ship The Commodore in 1897, about 10 miles off the coast from the Mosquito Inlet Lighthouse. With him were three men in a 10-foot boat. Try that sometime in the Atlantic Ocean if you don't care about drowning or sea-sickness. (See the excerpt at the front of this book.) Apparently, just before landing, the dinghy sank, and the men were tossed into the Atlantic, swimming the last length to safety. During the swim, one of the four men was lost.

The Mosquito Inlet Lighthouse helped Crane and the others to reach the shore, although it appeared to him to be just a pinprick from the bobbing sea. His shipwreck experience is captured forever in the short story "The Open Boat," frequently anthologized. Being saved from drowning, however, was but a short salvation for Crane, who died only three years later, at the age of 28, from tuberculosis.

Crane himself was from New York, one of 14 children born to Methodist missionaries. Crane's lady friend and long-term companion (if you can call anything long term in a life so short) was from Jacksonville. He met Cora Stewart after spending time in Cuba as a correspondent during the Spanish-American conflict. She would be considered his common-law wife. They met in 1896 at the Hotel de Dream brothel, which she owned.

"LOOK OUT NOW! STEADY, THERE!"

The captain, rearing cautiously in the bow after the dinghy soared on a great swell, said that he had seen the lighthouse at Mosquito Inlet. Presently the cook remarked that he had seen it. The correspondent was at the oars then, and for some reason he too wished to look at the lighthouse; but his back was toward the far shore, and the waves were important, and for some time he could not seize an opportunity to turn his head. But at last there came a wave more gentle than the others, and when at the crest of it he swiftly scoured the western horizon.

"See it?" said the captain.

"No," the correspondent said, slowly: "I didn't see anything."

"Look again," said the captain. He pointed. "It's exactly in that direction."

At the top of another wave the correspondent did as he was bid, and this time his eyes chanced on a small, still thing on the edge of the swaying horizon. It was precisely like the point of a pin. It took an anxious eye to find a lighthouse so tiny.

"Think we'll make it, Captain?"

"If the wind holds and the boat don't swamp, we can't do much else."

Stephen Crane, "The Open Boat"

THE NAME OF THE STORM

Early tropical storms and hurricanes were not named. A storm in the 1800s might be referred to as The Great Hurricane of 1848. In the 1920s, storms were sometimes named for the date they struck, such as The Labor Day Hurricane.

Military phonetics were used for naming of tropical storms and hurricanes beginning in 1953. Thus there could be tropical storm or Hurricane Able, Baker, Charlie, Delta, etc. It was, for example, Hurricane Easy striking Cedar Key with tremendous damage. Hurricane Easy was the first named hurricane. Proper names are now used to name storms. Thus there are hurricanes Arlene or Katrina. Because some letters are hard to match names to, the letters Q, U, X, Y, and Z are not used.

For a long time only women's names were used for tropical storms and hurricanes. However, in a age of greater awareness, this was deemed rather sexist, implying that only women were stormy. Now in equality, a Hurricane Andrew struck Florida in 1992.

If the letters of the alphabet are used up for a year, the current practice is to use the Greek alphabet, thus Hurricanes Alpha, Beta, etc. This occurred for the first time in 2005, the most active hurricane and tropical-storm season ever. Some storms, such as Hurricane Andrew, are so horrendous that their names are retired and never used again. This will likely be true for Hurricane Katrina.

PORT BOCA GRANDE LIGHTHOUSES
(Charlotte and Lee counties)

County boundaries are often weird in Florida. The boundaries are even stranger for islands, for example Anclote and Egmont keys, both of which have lighthouses. For example, a boundary divides Gasparilla Island, so that the lighthouses are in Lee County, while most of the island lies in Charlotte.

The current proper names for the lighthouses are Port Boca Grande Lighthouse and Gasparilla Island Light. To confuse the reader of lighthouse books, the Port Boca Grande Lighthouse was formerly the Gasparilla Island Lighthouse, sometimes also referred to as Old Port Boca Grande Island Lighthouse. The rear-range light previously was Garsparilla Island Rear-Range Lighthouse. The name changed from Gasparilla Island to Port Boca Grande a few decades ago when shoreline erosion threatened the lighthouse. The light was moved to a nearby, modern, skeleton tower. Normal Coast Guard practice would be to revert to the original name when the light was moved back to the dwelling tower, its original location, but this was not done.

These two, quite different lighthouses, have in common that they show the way to safety in an area with vigorous currents and substantial shoals. On some blustery days, whitecaps crossing the shallows are visible from shore.

Port Boca Grande Lighthouse is atop a building at the southern tip of Gasparilla Island looking across Boca Grande ("Big Mouth") Pass toward Cayo Costa ("Coast Key"). The lighthouse is described by the Coast Guard as "an octagonal tower on a square house." This lighthouse is at Lighthouse Beach Park and is part of Gasparilla Island State Park, which allows beach access to the public on an island that has sprouted with dwellings.

Inside the Port Boca Grande Lighthouse is the Boca Grande Lighthouse Museum. This is a first-class operation and one of the many reasons to visit.

The Gasparilla Island Light (or Boca Grande Entrance Rear-Range Light) is located perhaps a half-mile away from the house-like lighthouse. The rear-range light is on top of a skeletal tower with a enclosed central column and stairway. The lights pulse differently so they can be separated by boaters entering the harbor. The height from mean high water to focal plane is 105 feet.

Port Boca Grande Lighthouse is so very house-like in construction that it was once used as a home, and it is not at all evocative of a great, conical tower. It's distant relative is located in Cedar Keys National Wildlife Refuge on Seahorse Key. The building on top of which the light sits is only 44 feet high, the focal plane 41.

Originally the building included two bedrooms, a kitchen, a parlor, and a sitting room. An additional structure served as quarters for the assistant keeper. The lighthouse building is the oldest building on the island and was originally known as Gasparilla Island Light Station.

The rear-range light looks more like what we think of as a traditional lighthouse. It towers over a fine stretch of public beach where bathers enjoy the surf, sun, and all the gentle pleasures of idling away a few hours or a day at the beach.

According to "*The Florida Lighthouse Trail,* the rear-range light saw earlier service in Delaware.

Gasparilla Island Causeway, which allows visitors to reach the island, was built in 1957, but the first lighthouse was built long before that. The discovery of easily-mined phosphate in and along the Peace River in 1881 started the phosphate industry in the late 1800s. A railroad was built to the port in 1897 to support shipping of the phosphate rock.

At the beginning of the phosphate boom, more than 100 companies scurried to rip rock from the ground, including some nuggets from the bottom of the Peace River itself. All these little companies are gone. Currently two remain in Central Florida: perhaps the world's largest, privately-held corporation, Cargill, while a farmer's co-op, CF Industries, owns the other mining operations. IMC Phosphates, which absorbed Agrico, and became a separate company, was in recent years absorbed by Cargill, and the whole phosphate company operations are now under a company named Mosaic.

There are many things to be said about Boca Grande. One is tarpon fishing. Every year an annual tarpon tournament draws out competing anglers.

Another thing worthy of mention is pirate lore. Jose Gaspar, who is universally beloved and totally nonexistent, gives his name to the island. The wife of Gaspar, Joseffa, allegedly inspired the name of Useppa Island, now an exclusive community in the Gulf of Mexico. Although the pirate was a product of myth, not of flesh and blood, not even based on a real person, but started by a fictitious account in advertising brochures intended to dramatize the area, to this day, romance fanciers continue to describe his exploits as if they really happened.

In Tampa, there is an annual Gasparilla Day Festival during which the movers and shakers of the city revel and engage in bad behavior (recently rendered somewhat more civilized). The culmination of Gasparilla is the surrender of the city of Tampa to the pirates, and while this is allegedly a repeat of an actual event, it never happened. Of course, Gasparilla Island is said to have been the base of Pirate Gaspar's operations, perhaps the place where he buried his treasure. Not too long ago, locals sold treasure maps to Yankees for kicks and profit.

The pass between Boca Grande, a city on Gasparilla Island, and the island of Cayo Costa, where there is another marvelous state park, has vigorous tides. Cayo Costa State Park offers popular beach camping in limited numbers. This pass at Boca Grande is one entrance to Charlotte Harbor. The riptide is significant and can be witnessed from the southern tip of Gasparilla Island. Some sea kayakers have passed between Gasparilla Island and Cayo Costa; not a bad trip on a pleasant day, but sometimes exceptionally challenging and certainly not for everyone.

Another thing to mention is iguanas. Iguanas? Yes. What can be mistaken for a small alligator walking a lonely part of the beach is probably a lizard that's native land is Mexico. Within a few minutes, a visitor might count twenty or more iguanas scampering on the sand and within the brush. Apparently captive-bred iguanas have escaped and become wild on the island, although plans are underway to reverse the situation. A recent newspaper report put the iguana population on the island at several thousand.

By some reports, when lit in 1932, the rear-range possessed a range light, similar to a locomotive light. According to other sources, it was lighted by a fourth-order Fresnel. In current times, it uses modern optics, at the time of writing a Tidelands 250 Beacon. It casts a red light which flashes in a 6-second pattern of red and white. The architect and lens manufacturer for the rear-range light are unknown, but the builder was Phoenix Iron Company, Trenton, New Jersey.

The original Fresnel lens for the house-like Port Boca Grande Lighthouse was a third-and-a-half order which revolved. This order is one often used on lakes, such as the Great Lakes. The current light uses a 300-mm drum lens, that is a lens shaped like a drum. (A drum lens produces a light which might be described as all around, thus eliminating the need to rotate.) Its white light is interrupted every 4 seconds. The architect and lens manufacturer for the both lighthouses are unknown. While the builder of the Port Boca Grande Lighthouse is unknown, Gasparilla Island Light's (the

rear-range) tower has been reported as built by Phoenix Iron Company of Trenton, New Jersey, although some lighthouse experts doubt this.

The lighthouses went out of service in 1966, and then they were re-commissioned in 1986. Built in 1890, Port Boca Grande Lighthouse was placed in the National Register of Historic Places 90 years later in 1980.

Top: Boca Grande's "house-like" lighthouse.

Above: One of Gasparilla Island's population of iguanas which descended from escaped pets.

Right: Turbulent seas at Boca Grande (near the entrance to Charlotte Harbor) give visitors some indication of why a lighthouse was built in this location.

Port Boca Grande Lighthouses

THE VOICE OF A LIGHTHOUSE

The sound most associated with a lighthouse is the deep booming of a foghorn. Although Florida fogs can be as thick as those anywhere, not a lot of foghorns were ever used in the Sunshine State. Egmont Key Lighthouse once had a hand-held fog horn that was later replaced with a fog bell, later discontinued. Volusia Bar Lighthouse also had a fog signal at one time.

IMPORTANT DATES

1881 Phosphate Discovered in the Peace River Drainage

1890 Lighthouse Lighted (December 31)

1897-8 Railroad and Facilities Built

1918 Rear-range Light Discontinued in Delaware

1921 Funding for Rear-range Light

1932 Rear-range Lighted

1956 Port Boca Grande Lighthouse Automated

1957 Bridge Construction Starts

1966 Light Removed

1967 Coast Guard Abandoned the Lighthouse

1980 Placed on National Register of Historic Places

1986 Coast Guard Re-commissions Lighthouse

1988 Gasparilla Island State Recreation Area Created
(The SRA designation has since been dropped by the State of Florida.)

DIRECTIONS

From I-75 south of Sarasota, exit on River Road toward the Gulf. After about 7 miles, there is a light at US-41. Cross US-41 where the road name changes. Turn south on CR-775, and after several miles, turn southwest on CR-771. This a toll bridge onto the island. The bridges are narrow, and there are bicyclists, walkers, and joggers, so use caution. Once actually on the island, turn right at the stop sign, and follow the winding road. The rear-range light will soon be seen, and at the end of the road lies the Lighthouse Museum and Port Boca Grande Lighthouse. There are excellent displays within the museum, which is closed during the month of August. Bring swimming suit, sun-tan lotion, and some water. Also some cash for the toll bridge, parking stickers, a donation for the museum, and perhaps to buy some of the fine lighthouse items sold by the gift shop.

Top, left: The rear range light at Boca Grande. In the past, mariners would line up this light with another light located in the water in order to place their vessel in the approach channel. (See chart on page 33)

PULASKI SHOAL LIGHT
(Monroe County)

Pulaski Shoal Light has a Coast Guard height from mean high water to the focal plane of 49 feet. It is described as a hexagonal, pyramidal, skeleton tower on piles. It was located 30 miles northwest of Key West and built in 1935. The shoal may have been named for a shipwreck, a vessel of the Center Line of New York that sank in 1832. The light flashes white every 6 seconds and is visible for 9 miles. Casimir Pulaski was a Polish general who fought in the American Revolution, as a result of which his name blesses many cities and apparently the boat for which the shoal is named. Many sources report the tower as non-operational or even fallen; however, it is on the 2007 Coast Guard Light List.

REBECCA SHOAL LIGHTHOUSE
(Monroe County)

The story of Rebecca Shoal Lighthouse is one of storms, hardships, and difficulty. These three qualities may apply to many lighthouses and particularly the offshore reef lighthouses, but they are fitting for Rebecca Shoal. Compared to the other offshore lighthouses, this one has had a hard time standing.

There has been a day beacon and a lighthouse, and several attempts to build both at Rebecca Shoal, which is located 43 miles from Key West in the general direction of the Dry Tortugas. The day beacon stood 75 feet, shipped from Key West, and built on Rebecca Shoal in 1879. The first lighthouse was lighted on November 1, 1886, and had a house-like structure atop iron screw-piles with a black lantern. The

three keepers were no longer required when the light was automated in 1925. The empty quarters remained on Rebecca Shoal until 1953, when the dwelling was demolished because of the deteriorated condition and replaced by a simple wooden lattice tower. In 1985, deterioration of the iron foundation piles caused the entire structure to be demolished and replaced by a modern light tower with no dwelling. The structure of a lighthouse on this shoal was severely damaged, by all reports, in 2004 when a number of hurricanes passed through the area, including Hurricane Charley. The structure is apparently damaged and non-operational as of writing. Some reports are that it is down completely. It remains on the Coast Guard Light List, which would indicate it may operate again someday.

Initial efforts by Lieutenant George Meade to build the lighthouse failed. An epidemic, slow appropriations, weather, and Meade's attentions to Sombrero Key Lighthouse all combined to provide delays, until a hurricane came along in 1858 to set the project back to square one when it annihilated the construction. As reported in *Florida Lighthouse Trail*, Meade said that Rebecca Shoal Lighthouse was attempted under greater obstacles and with more exposure than any other lighthouse. The Civil War was a substantial obstacle also.

Life must have been tough on Rebecca Shoal. Waves and wind caused damage that keepers dealt with in improvised means. It was a long cruise from Key West or from the Dry Tortugas. There was no shelter in

storms. How hard life may have been could be illustrated this way: In 1902, Keeper Jasper Walker jumped off the lighthouse in an apparent suicide. Walker was reported in an agitated and exhausted state, making an accident seem unlikely.

The Coast Guard Light List gives the height at 66 feet. It was originally lighted by a fourth-order Fresnel lens, but later used a Amerace 190-mm Beacon, which rotated, and a 250-mm lantern, both powered by sunlight. Originally it flashed red and white every 6 seconds; this was later changed to white with one red sector from 254 to 302 degrees to indicate the dangerous reef. The architect, builder, lens maker, and number of steps in the original lighthouse are unknown.

IMPORTANT DATES
1854	Day Beacon Construction
1855	Storm Destroyed Day Beacon
1873	Day Beacon Completed (May) Storm Destroyed Day Beacon (October)
1886	Day Beacon Erected
1886	Rebecca Shoal Lighthouse Operational
1889	Storm Damages Lens
1893	Light Pattern Changed
1902	Lighthouse Keeper Committed Suicide
1925	Lighthouse Automated
1953	House Removed
1985	New Tower Built
2004	Hurricane Season Brought Damage

ST. AUGUSTINE LIGHTHOUSE
(St. Johns County)

This is one of Florida's premier lighthouses. The visitor can experience this lighthouse both within and without, and it is impressive. From short trails through the woods, it can be seen towering into the sky, while the interior is as amazing a sight as the exterior's black candy stripe and the red observation deck about the lens.

From atop the structure, one sight the visitor can see is a 208-foot tall cross, made of stainless steel, erected and marking the first American city established in 1565. St. Augustine is a history-rich area, because it has been inhabited so long, and is America's oldest existing city. Very few places in North America even come close to having such a rich history. More than a half-century before Pilgrims descended on Plymouth Rock, European powers were contesting St. Augustine. Historic places abound, including Fort Caroline. Sir Francis Drake, the English buccaneer, burned the city to the ground in 1586, four-and-a-half centuries ago.

Within the lighthouse from the bottom of the stairwell, the visitor can gaze up at 219 dizzying, spiraling, metal steps. The metal handrail trails off into the heights. Lighthouse literature points out that walking to the top is like climbing a 14-story building. Gazing upward from the bottom, it is possible to conjure up the fear of vertigo, and walking up the steps is a little like working out. Many visitors pause at the bottom of the stairwell to consider. Fortunately, there are nine steel landings where it possible to rest and catch one's breath. These landings also come in handy when encountering folks climbing in the opposite direction for the steps are not wide and one-person-at-a-time between landings is more comfortable.

The original 39-foot lighthouse, built of coquina in 1824, was destroyed when erosion caused its collapse in 1880. The height was raised to 52 feet in 1852 before its demise.

Amelia Island lays claim to being the oldest lighthouse in Florida. It was built in 1820, but it was built in Georgia, and moved to Florida after the first St. Augustine Lighthouse was built. The St. Augustine site has been occupied by lighthouses longer than Ameila, by a few years.

Some historians believe that the foundation beneath the original lighthouse served as the base for at least two Spanish watchtowers. Spanish watchtowers in the area date back to the 1500s. It is likely the Spanish placed a beacon on one or more of the watchtowers, truly making it Florida's first lighthouse. This would predate even the first colonial lighthouse in Boston.

The original St. Augustine Lighthouse was abandoned in 1874, six years before its collapse, when the current lighthouse was built. From the observation deck of the current lighthouse it is possible to see the site of the original lighthouse. Before that first lighthouse collapsed, it was equipped in 1858 with a fourth-order Fresnel lens.

Like other Florida lights, St. Augustine Lighthouse was darkened during the Civil War by sabotage, and lit after the war was over.

The web site (see Appendix A) for the St. Augustine Lighthouse states the present lighthouse was built of Alabama brick, Georgia granite, and Philadelphia iron. Whatever it is built of, it is a beautiful sight, and the view from its top is sublime.

It is an active lighthouse, in more ways than one. Each year thousands of visitors arrive to take in the sight and climb the steps. And they should come. Not only is it a splendid sight, the St. Augustine Lighthouse is a survivor. It has taken rare Florida earthquakes, hurricanes, fires, lightning strikes, and bullet wounds to its eye, while about it humans have suffered epidemics and wars.

Approaching the lighthouse from the parking lot, it is impossible to see the whole structure for the trees and power lines. It is necessary to get up close to see the stone tower's base and top at the same time without obstructions.

The original first-order Fresnel lens is still installed in the lighthouse. The light is fixed and white, with a single flash every 30 seconds, and comes from a lighthouse 167 feet tall with a focal plane of 168 feet. The architect was Paul J. Pelz, the builder, Paulding, Kemble and Company, of Cold Springs, New York, and the Fresnel lens was manufactured by L. Sautter et Limonier.

IMPORTANT DATES

1565 St. Augustine Founded by Pedro Menendez de Aviles
1586 Sir Francis Drake Burns the City
1824 Original Lighthouse Built - Lit April 5
1848 Lighthouse Height Extended
1852 Lighthouse Raised to 52 Feet
1858 Fourth-order Fresnel Installed
1862 Lens Re-installed
1867 Lighthouse Re-lit
1874 New Lighthouse Lighted (October 15)
      Old Lighthouse Abandoned
1879 Charleston Earthquake Felt in Tower
1880 Original Lighthouse Topples into the Sea

1885 Fuel Changed from Lard to Kerosene
1909 Incandescent Oil Vapor Lamp Installed
1936 Lighthouse Electrified
1955 Automated
1980 Restoration Efforts Begin
1981 Placed on the National Register of Historic Places
1988 Museum Opened
2000 Visitors' Center Opened

DIRECTIONS

The lighthouse and museum are open to the public. In St. Augustine, take A1A across the Bridge of the Lions. Very shortly, the lighthouse will be evident on the left. Down the road lies Anastasia State Park, a land of sand dunes and beach flowers.

Top: The magnificent "candy-striped" St. Augustine Lighthouse faces the Atlantic Ocean.

ST. JOHNS LIGHTHOUSE
(Duval County)

Two lighthouses are located on Mayport Naval Station. The lighthouse above and the lighthouses on the opposie page are popularly known as the Mayport Lighthouse, or lighthouses, because they are located aboard the station, near the community of Mayport; which is east of Jacksonville, and at the mouth of the St. Johns River and the Atlantic Ocean. Little Talbot Island lies to the north on the coast.

In 1565, Mayport was the site of a French Huguenot settlement. While the term originally was more specific to one group, the word Huguenot by then meant French Protestants in general. A small number of Frenchmen and a handful of Spaniards contested in the New World for a land full of Native Americans. In general, French efforts in Florida failed for many reasons, including poor supply and the massacre of French captives and Captain Jean Ribaut at Mantanzas (place of slaughter).

Like the St. Johns River Lighthouse, St. Johns Lighthouse is currently aboard Mayport Naval Air Station, established during World War II. The military, at present, does not allow civilians on the base except on rare occasions.

In 2005, members of the Florida Lighthouse Association were allowed onboard. Perhaps the best way to see these lighthouses is to join the association and wait for the next tour unless base policy changes. Joining the association is a great way to bolster lighthouse preservation anyway and contacts are in Appendix A.

In books in print, there exists some imprecision in naming the two St. Johns lighthouses. Sometimes the term "light station" is applied to both lighthouses. A station implies one or more dwellings in association with a lighthouse, but this is not a hard and fast rule. Since both the St. Johns River Lighthouse and St. Johns Lighthouse had dwellings, they both technically are light stations, although the dwellings are no longer lived in or have disappeared completely.

This lighthouse is a modern structure, built at a cost of $250,000 in 1954, and stands 64 feet, with a focal plane of 80 feet. In appearance, it does not look like a traditional lighthouse. One lighthouse enthusiast described it as an "art deco" lighthouse. It is also described as art deco in the *Florida Lighthouse Trail.*

When built, the St. Johns Lighthouse also had a radio beacon in addition to its light, and it took the place of the St. Johns Lightship, stationed 7 miles at sea in the Atlantic Ocean. Originally powered by a FB-61A Beacon, the current device is a Vega VRB-25 Beacon, which sends out four white flashes every 20 seconds. The architect and builder are unknown.

DIRECTIONS

Mayport Naval Station is on the south side of the mouth of the St. Johns River at the dead-end of A1A. This lighthouse, however, is not visible from A1A. It can be seen from the water or the end of the last coastal road approaching Mayport Naval Station, although it may be hard to distinguish from the other buildings.

Top: St. Johns Lighthouse as seen from the ocean on a windy, stormy day.

ST. JOHNS RIVER LIGHTHOUSE
(Duval County)

The St. Johns River is the longest river in Florida at 273 miles. It's more than a river, though. It is a conglomeration of water bodies. Native Americans named the river *Welaka*, or chain of lakes. Wide spots include Lakes George, Harney, Jessup, Monroe, Norris, and Blue Cypress, among others. (Lake George is Florida's second-largest lake, after Lake Okeechobee, and once had its own lighthouse: Volusia Bar Lighthouse. Lake Okeechobee had a number of unmanned towers also.) From Palatka north, the river is considered a marine estuary, and there is even a species of shark that enters it at times.

While the southern interior of the river is, in many sections, at times too shallow for big boats, the mouth of the St. Johns is one-half mile wide and a challenge to navigate, especially before the shipping channel was dredged. Hence the need for the lighthouses at the river's Atlantic mouth.

Spanish explorers named the St. Johns *Rio de Corrientes* (river of currents) undoubtedly for the river mouth, which rises and falls with the tides, as farther south the river barely has current at times. The French called it the May River, because they began exploring it in May, but it was the Spanish mission of *San Juan de Puerto* that gave St. Johns its name. The *Rio de Corrientes* designation was apparently also used at Canaveral.

Two previous towers did not work out. According to *Florida Lighthouse Trail*, the first two lighthouses failed because the places where they were located allowed erosion to become a problem.

The 1858 lighthouse was first lighted with a third-order Fresnel lens which did not rotate. It shown forth in a fixed white light with a red sector. A red, cone-shaped tower, the lighthouse is 80 feet tall with a 77-foot focal plane. The architect, builder, and manufacturer of the Fresnel lens are all unknown.

DIRECTIONS

The old lighthouse is on the north side of the base near the ferry dock in Mayport.

IMPORTANT DATES

1829 Congress Appropriates $10,550 for Lighthouse
1830 First Lighthouse Built
1835 Lighthouse Replaced and Relocated
1858-9 Third Lighthouse Built
1859 Operational January 1
1860 Civil War Interrupts Operations Keeper Damages Lens
1867 Relighted July 4
1887 Lighthouse Height Increased
1920 Electrified
1929 Lightship Replaces Lighthouse
1941 Mayport Naval Station Built
1954 St. Johns Lighthouse Built
1967 Lighthouse Automated
1982 1858 Lighthouse Placed on National Registry of Historic Places
1997 Mayport Lighthouse Association Forms

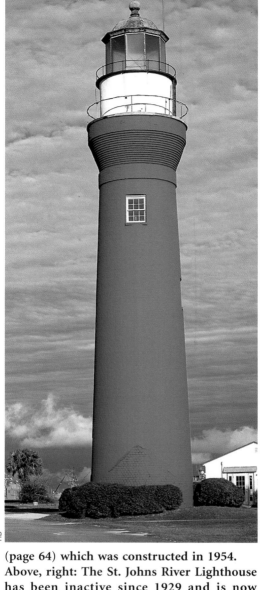

Above, left: The St. Johns Lightship replaced the St. Johns River Lighthouse in 1929. Its floating light guided ships to the river's mouth until replaced by the St. Johns Lighthouse (page 64) **which was constructed in 1954. Above, right: The St. Johns River Lighthouse has been inactive since 1929 and is now maintained as an historical building.**

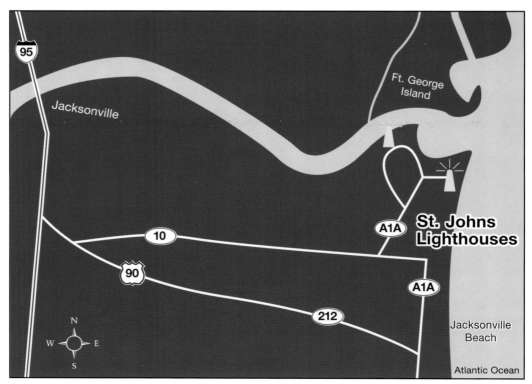

ST. JOSEPH LIGHTHOUSES
(Gulf County)

St. Joseph Bay is formed by the mainland, where the City of Port St. Joe is located, and St. Joseph Peninsula. The result looks on the map like a weirdly long arm signaling a left-hand turn. The "arm" extends in a protective parallel to the mainland. The bay mouth is narrow, and the bay seems very protected from the elements, but this was not always true, as witnessed by the fate of a city facing hurricanes referred to as "The Wrath of God."

The southerly portions of the bay are quite shallow. At the northerly mouth of the bay, however, there was depth sufficient for Spanish explorers to sail into the bay that some believe to be named after the husband of Mary, mother of Jesus. The local historical society believes the name may derive from the date the Spanish discovered it, that it was named for the patron saint of that day. The depth has been changed since those days by hurricanes. The bay was an important port supporting commerce and settlement in the area. It modern times, the bay is pristine and a pleasure to boat and particularly to kayak.

The first lighthouse, built to support shipping and commerce, was known as the St. Joseph Bay Lighthouse, even though it was located on St. Joseph Point, at the very tip of St. Joseph Peninsula. This area is now within St. Joseph Peninsula State Park.

After the destruction of the first brick-tower lighthouse by The Great Middle Florida Hurricane of August 1851, the second lighthouse built was located on the mainland and faced the bay opening. Perversely, the lighthouse on the mainland was designated the St. Joseph Point Lighthouse and the St. Joseph Point Light Range Station.

Construction on the first lighthouse is said to have been begun in 1838. This is an important date in Florida history, for Florida's Constitutional Convention was held in Port St. Joe during that year. The lighthouse was completed as 1839.

Hurricanes and disease combined in a manner that must have seemed to the inhabitants of Port St. Joe to literally have been the wrath of God. Storms and plague not only destroyed the first lighthouse and people who could care for it and man it, they also forced the virtual abandonment of the city of Port St. Joe.

The dates for these events are all over the place in books in print. Variously the hurricane is said to have occurred in 1841, 1842, 1847, and 1848. In the case of hurricanes, perhaps this is because that area of the Gulf Coast usually feels some effects

from a hurricane in every hurricane season. The other calamity, yellow fever, is variously stated in other books as occurring in 1841, 1842, and 1847, and perhaps the town experienced more than one bout of yellow fever, as the disease was prevalent then.

However, it is clear that in 1840, the schooner *Herald* from The Greater Antilles arrived with sailors suffering from yellow fever. Within four days, the *Herald* sailed on for Havana but left its sick in Port St. Joe. In 1841, there was a yellow fever epidemic, then the hurricane.

Two factors combine to spread yellow fever in the Northern Hemisphere: mosquitos and men. In the Southern Hemisphere, monkeys can take the place of men, but there are few monkeys in North America, none native. The two types of yellow fever are described as jungle and urban. In modern times, the yellow fever mosquito (*Aedes aegypti*) has been eliminated from North America. It was not so in 1840 and 1841.

The cause and effect between the *Herald* and the epidemic seems unclear. This is an account from *The Star of Florida*: "Daily (rain) showers had filled the noisome marshes....Swarms of mosquitos rose from their many breeding places...One morn the news arrived that there had been a death from yellow fever. Bankers ceased counting money....Other days passed and more deaths were announced...Uncontrollable fear seized upon all."

"Yellow Jack," as the settlers called it, along with the help of hurricanes, would reduce a town of 5,000 to 500 through death and evacuation. Eventually the town was abandoned.

Like hepatitis, the disease of yellow fever causes the skin to take on a yellow cast. It was a deadly disease, especially in those times, accompanied by headaches, high fevers, and vomiting. It laid low Port St. Joe like the plague it was.

According to some accounts, the yellow-fever outbreak was followed by a tidal wave. This is almost certainly not true. There are no reports of it. The geology of the region is not such that such an catastrophic event, a *tsunami*, would be expected, although occasional rogue waves have surprised shipping in the Gulf on rare occasions. Also, given the protective, mostly-enclosed bay, such a rarity would have had to been focused right into the bay mouth.

That's just what a hurricane did that swept away most of St. Joseph following widespread illness. To this day, at low tide, one can wander onto the foundation of buildings in the bay and dig up artifacts, like plates, cups, silverware, knives, and stones. The hurricane or hurricanes, which struck Port St. Joe, came at it from the very worst possible direction for the settler residents - the west.

A monstrous wall of tidal surge, called *The Great Tide* in a fictional book of the 1930s, rose up over the coastal city and rolled over it, probably extending inland some distance. It moved sand and changed the channels within the bay as it decimated the lives of the settlers.

The second, house-like lighthouse became operational in 1902. It was very house-like in appearance and is, in fact, the current residence of Danny Raffield, who helped the author with this account. Mr. Raffield is a fourth-generation, Gulf County

resident, and he wrote the account for the St. Joseph Point Lighthouse for *The Florida Lighthouse Trail*. The optical device was a third-order Fresnel lens, which is now located in the Gulf County Public Library in Port St. Joe. The light was fixed and did not rotate. In print, there are likewise disputing dates about when the lighthouse closed, 1955 and 1960. It was certainly unmanned in 1952.

According to Mr. Raffield, the second lighthouse had a range light. When sailors at sea first saw a light, the distance was usually 13 miles. As vessels prepared to enter St. Joseph Bay, from 6 miles out, the range light helped keep them off the shoals near Mexico Beach.

The house is now located southeast of Port St. Joe. No beacon shines forth, nor is it open to the public in any sense, although it is possible to drive by and gaze upon it in appreciation. After the lighthouse was closed, it was sold and first moved to Mexico Beach and then to its current location. The dates provided below are those from *Florida Lighthouse Trail*, where Mr. Raffield's account can be read.

The architect and builder are unknown. The third-order Fresnel lens was manufactured by Barbier, Bernard et Turenne. Directions

DIRECTIONS

The building is located on the coastal side of SR-30A at Simmons Bayou, a small community west of Apalachicola and south of Port St. Joe.

IMPORTANT DATES

1837	Funds for Lighthouse Appropriated
1838	Florida's Constitutional Convention Lighthouse Construction Begins
1839	Lighthouse Construction Complete (February 23)
1841	Yellow Fever Outbreak September Hurricane
1843	Lighthouse Abandoned September Hurricane
1844	August Hurricane
1846	Lighthouse Decommissioned
1901	Congress Funds New Lighthouse
1902	New Lighthouse Operational
1952	Lighthouse Unmanned
1955	Lighthouse Replaced with Automated Tower
1960	Lighthouse Sold as Surplus

Opposite page: St. Joseph Point Lighthouse shown in black and white when it was operational. This lighthouse operated with a range light which helped incoming vessels avoid Mexico Shoals. The main light was visible 13 miles at sea and helped ships in finding the bay entrance.

Top: The lighthouse has become a private residence and is not open to the public although it is clearly visible from the highway just south of Port St. Joe.

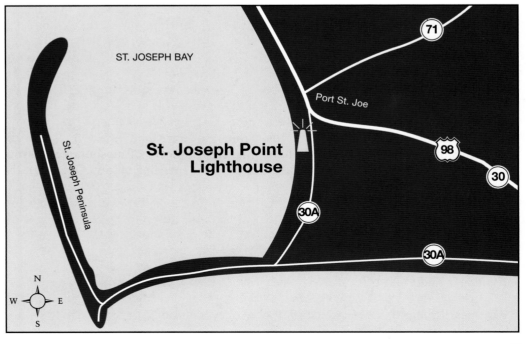

ST. MARKS LIGHTHOUSE
(Wakulla County)

St. Marks Lighthouse is located near Newport, Florida, within St. Marks National Wildlife Refuge, where it looks out on the Gulf of Mexico. Hiking trails nearby it provide ample opportunity for viewing the lighthouse from every angle except from the water. A nearby boat ramp provides that opportunity, for visitors with a boat or a kayak.

St. Marks is also the beginning of the Big Bend Saltwater Paddling Trail, which now stretches to Yankeetown, one of the state's designated canoe-and-kayak recreational trails.

The town of St. Marks, its two wonderful, rustic seafood restaurants, and its bed and breakfast, were flooded by Hurricane Dennis in 2005. From the Big Bend to Port St. Joe, an unexpected tidal surge swamped everything in its path close to the water, including portions of the Refuge. The lighthouse lost a glass panel, but water did not enter it, and there was no major damage.

St. Marks Wildlife Refuge around the lighthouse is itself is a wonderful place to visit, including parts of the Florida Trail, on which wildlife is easily seen. Wild turkeys often scamper across the trail. Deer are frequently seen. There is even a reasonable chance of seeing Florida black bears within the Refuge. The Refuge has a first-class visitor center and a helpful staff, but it does not allow overnight camping.

Spanish influence in the area can be dated as far back as 1528 when Panfilo de Narvaez arrived with three hundred men. They built boats with which they attempted to sail to Mexico. In 1539, Hernando de Soto and six hundred men wintered in what is now Tallahassee. DeSoto's supply ships came from Tampa Bay to the St. Marks River. The river was marked by two yellow banners hung from trees. Around 1650, the river mouth (where the St. Marks and Wakulla rivers join) was used as a port for Mission San Luis. A wooden fort was built there in 1679-80, and subsequently burned down by pirates in 1682. In 1718, Spanish soldiers, led by a Captain Jose Primo de Ribera, arrived to construct a second fort. The town of St. Marks came into being in March of 1718, possibly on the Feast Day of St. Mark, an apostle, hence the probable origin of the name.

The original lighthouse, apparently unsatisfactorily built by Benjamin Beal and Jurius Taylor in 1828, was finished in 1830 and quickly replaced in 1831. The collector of customs, one Jesse Willis, refused to accept the lighthouse because of hollow walls. Willis was not familiar with this design and wanted more substantial walls. A second lighthouse was built by Calvin Knowlton. The location for this lighthouse proved problematic because of erosion, thus the second lighthouse was relocated, according to the Refuge.

During the Civil War, many of the lighthouses in the south had their lenses destroyed or stolen. This was the easiest and quickest way to put a lighthouse out of commission. Often this was done by rebel sympathizers. Lenses were expensive, took time to make and transport, and were difficult to move.

Not only did the Confederates disable the lighthouse at St. Marks, in 1865, one side or the other may have attempted to blowup it up. Some historians doubt this event. This is a relatively small structure, and one would think it would not be too hard to destroy it if one had sufficient powder. It also looks like it would be easy to burn. Thankfully, if there was an attempt to blow the lighthouse, the term SNAFU is older than the 20th century.

The original Fresnel lens was removed by Confederates during the war. Its fate is unknown. A Fresnel lens was reinstalled in 1866. Some accounts give this as 1867.

Originally lighted with 15 Lewis lamps and 14-inch reflectors, a fourth-order Fresnel lens is presently used. The light is in a very house-like structure, made of wood, stone, and masonry. There are 80 steps in the 88-foot lighthouse, which has a focal plane of 82 feet. A white light shines forth, occluded every 4 seconds. The architect was Winslow Lewis. The fourth-order Fresnel lens replacing the Lewis lamps was manufactured by Henri-LePaute.

While there is no museum or gift shop at the lighthouse, the headquarters at St. Marks National Wildlife Refuge has an excellent gift shop.

DIRECTIONS

The Refuge is a southerly turn in Newport from US-98, just east of the bridge over the St. Marks River, and clearly marked with signs. Newport is to the west of Perry and south of Tallahassee. Along US-98, which is the road nearest the Refuge, a considerable amount of land is either in the Refuge, wildlife management areas managed by the state, and (farther west and north) much land is within Apalachicola National Forest.

IMPORTANT DATES

1680 Spanish Fort
1718 St. Marks Established
1828-9 Lighthouse Built
1831 Second Lighthouse Built
1842 Lighthouse Moved to New Location
1843 Hurricane Destroys Quarters
1865 Confederates Substantially Damage Lighthouse
1867 Re-lighted Following Civil War
1931 St. Marks National Wildlife Refuge Established
1957 Lighthouse Automated

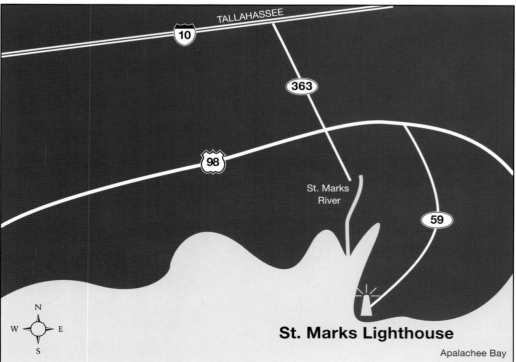

St. Marks Lighthouse

Apalachee Bay

SAND KEY LIGHTHOUSE
(Monroe County)

Applying the term "key" or "island" to Sand Key is a long reach. Hurricanes and more hurricanes have rearranged it, removed it, taken away and rebuilt it, over and over. Sand Key, at times, has lacked any sand, dispersed by the vigor of storm tides. Historically-documented rising sea levels apparently have nothing to do with this phenomena.

Englishmen left a day beacon at Sand Key in 1770, but it was more than a half-century before a lighthouse was built. That 63-foot brick lighthouse lasted 19 years, from 1827 to 1846. It was lighted by 14 lamps with 21-inch reflectors.

The Great Hurricane of 1846 that took down the brick lighthouse is the same October hurricane that at Key West Lighthouse drowned six of lighthouse keeper Barbara Mabrity's children and eight others when the tower collapsed. At Sand Key, there was no place else to take shelter but the lighthouse, and the surf undermined it, causing its collapse with the death of all six inside.

The first Sand Key Lighthouse also had a lady lighthouse keeper, Rebecca Flaherty. In both cases, the ladies assumed a job previously held by their husbands. Fortunately, Mrs. Flaherty remarried and was not in the tower at Sand Key when it came crashing down. Joshua Appleby and members of his family were not so fortunate.

After the first lighthouse was destroyed in the Great Hurricane of 1846, a hurricane predating modern record keeping, the Lightship *Honey* was posted in the area for seven years, while the second and present screw-pile lighthouse was under construction. The screw-pile design has stood the test of time and storms, and Sand Key Lighthouse is more than 150 years old.

The second Sand Key Lighthouse is moored not on the sand but into coral 10 feet below. Thirteen-foot piles were driven into the coral where a cement base was poured. The sand might wash out from under Sand Key Lighthouse, but that could no longer cause a collapse.

The 132-foot lighthouse has a focal plane of 109 feet, and was originally lighted by a first-order Fresnel lens. The lighthouse's 112 steps were destroyed by a fire in 1989. There have been a number of modern optical devices used. It is currently lighted by a Vega VRB-25 Beacon, which rotates and emits two white flashes every 15 seconds with two red sectors. The architect was I. W. P. Lewis; the builders J. V. Merrick and Son for the lantern and watch room and John F. Riley Ironworks of

Charleston, South Carolina; the Chief Engineer was Lieutenant George Meade; and the lens manufacturer Henri-LePuate.

In time a boathouse, dock, and weather station were built. The wooden keeper's quarters, stairs, and lantern room were destroyed during a fire in 1989. From 1989 to 1996, the lighthouse was deactivated while plans were made for its restoration.

IMPORTANT DATES

1770 British Day Beacon
1826 Funds Appropriated
1827 First Lighthouse Built
1846 First Lighthouse Destroyed
1846 Lightship *Honey* Deployed
1853 Second Lighthouse Lighted (July 20, 1853)
      Honey Re-deployed
1941 Light Automated
1953 Placed on National Register of Historic Places
1982 Fresnel Removed; Modern Optics Installed
1989 Fire at Lighthouse During Renovation
      Deactivated for Restoration
1996 Reactivated

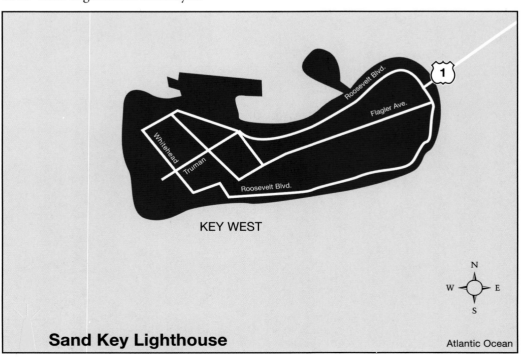

Sand Key Lighthouse

KEY WEST

Atlantic Ocean

CORAL REEFS IN THE KEYS

The coral reef landscape is a rich wonderland, full of multicolored fishes, perhaps 600 species or more. It is a national treasure. Florida's coral reefs stretch from near Miami at Fowey Rocks around Florida and west to the Dry Tortugas. They are the result of thousands of years of living and dying corals, built on countless trillions upon trillions of skeletal remains of earlier generations, with a living topping of coral creatures. How many reefs are there? Over 100 remain in the Keys, all delicate ecological treasures as endangered in their own way as the Florida panther.

Coral polyps gather calcium from the sea water. They use the calcium (much like kids use calcium from milk to grow bones) to compose their hard outer layer or skeleton. Some corals add as little as a half-inch per year to their skeletons, while staghorn coral grows up to four-inches per year.

All coral is endangered by the activities of man. For some species of coral, touching it is enough to kill it. Anchors are dragged across it, propellers strike it, for a time people carried it home to collect it. Perhaps the longest-term threat and most serious is from the polluted run-off from human activities.

Living coral requires a nutrient-poor environment. Off Florida's coastline, from the other Gulf coastal states, and out the mouth of the Mississippi River come tremendous amounts of nitrogen and phosphates from runoff fertilizers and airborne deposition. When a nutrient poor-environment is replaced with an enriched one, a lot of bad things can happen. Corals can themselves excrete a protective mucus, but at some point that can become harmful. Dissolved solids can lower oxygen in the water column, and corals, like fishes, need oxygen. Red tides and algae blooms can shade out life-giving sunlight. The length and frequency of red tide is increasing. Millions of pounds of nitrogen are entering the Gulf of Mexico (a lot from the Caloosahatchee and Peace rivers) and circulate right at the heart of some of these coral reefs.

Efforts to eliminate pollution runoff are admirable and have achieved much, but not enough. Too little action through another human lifetime could conceivably destroy the living coral reefs in the Keys. Once gone, it might be thousands of years, if ever, before they could be replaced.

WRECKER AND LIGHTHOUSE KEEPER

On October 10, 1846, the original Sand Key Lighthouse plunged into the sea. Joshua Appleby, his family and some visitors all perished.

Appleby led a hard-working and somewhat colorful life. In 1823, he was imprisoned for wrecking activities. Before becoming lighthouse keeper in 1837, he earned his living with catches from the sea and the contents of wrecks. At that time, he dwelled on Key Vaca. Today, a Coast Guard cutter is named in his honor.

WINSLOW LEWIS, LIGHTHOUSE ENTREPRENEUR

Winslow Lewis, of Wellfleet, Massachusetts, was a ship's captain, who was captured by the British during the War of 1812. Lewis (1770-1850) designed the so-called Lewis lamps, a system using whale-oil-fueled lights. The design borrowed from Aime Argand's Argand lamp from France. Lewis' lighting apparatus consisted of three parts: a reflector, an Argand lamp with a hollow wick, and a lens. The lens was ineffective and soon discontinued.

Lighthouses provided a steady source of income for Lewis and his company. Not only did Lewis supply the lamps, but he supplied whale oil as well, and built approximately 100 lighthouse towers, including the one at St. Marks.

Top: Sand Key Lighthouse plays an important role in the safe navigation of ships passing Key West. This view shows the lighthouse when the fire-damaged dwelling was still present.

Opposite Page: A more recent view of the lighthouse after it was deactivated.

SANIBEL ISLAND LIGHTHOUSE
(Lee County)

Although one wouldn't know it now for all the homes and high rises, Punta Rassa on San Carlos Harbor opposite Sanibel on the mainland was a booming port in the mid to late 1800s. It was also vital to the growth of the city of Fort Myers.

In hopes of more prosperity, Punta Rassa citizens lobbied for a lighthouse as early as the 1830s. While Punta Rassa was once a way station for cattle on the way to Cuba, it was also a popular fishing village. During the Civil War, Punta Rassa was home to Fort Delaney, a probably small and unimportant fort, which was established in 1837, and later abandoned. Today, fishing is still a recreational interest to many who live in the area.

Punta Rassa means "flat point" or "raveling point" in Spanish, and the land is certainly flat. In *Place Names of Florida* (Pineapple Press), it is theorized that from Punta Rassa the coastline of Sanibel appeared to be unraveling. Appropriate or not, it is a Spanish name which hung on, just as Sanibel or Sanybel is a corruption of some Spanish word or words we may never know. According to the same book, a Spanish map from 1768 designates the island Puerto de S. Nibel.

The beach by the lighthouse is a great place to spend a day. Sanibel is also a wonderful place to spend a long weekend. By the lighthouse, there is a short, sandy, public beach, while to the north there are weekend and weekly rentals of luxury condominiums. Once in a while, an uninformed European tourist makes a spectacular nude or semi-nude appearance. Otherwise, going to this beach is laid-back and unexciting. With luck, the visitor may see porpoise pods. At the right time of the year, stingrays appear in plentiful numbers, requiring bathers to either stay out of the water or do the stingray shuffle.

Not far from Sanibel Lighthouse is the Lighthouse Restaurant, where crowds often wait on Saturday and Sunday mornings to get a seafood omelet, among other fine things.

To the west on the island is J. N. "Ding" Darling National Wildlife Refuge. This is a excellent place to watch wildlife, particularly birds, and to bike and hike. Canoe trails exist at Tarpon Bay Recreation Area and Buck Key, and there are guided tours into Sanibel mangroves.

Sanibel Island Lighthouse was first lit on August 20, 1894, with a third-order Fresnel lens which revolved. It sent two white flashes every 6 seconds. In 1923, a second, third-order Fresnel went into use. In 1962, that Fresnel lens was replaced with a modern optic, a 500-mm Drum Lens. According to current Coast Guard information, the modern optic now in use is a Tidelands 300-mm Beacon. The manufacturers of the first Fresnel lens used was Henri-LePaute, but the manufacturer of the other lens is unknown. The tower is 112 feet tall, with a 98-foot focal plane, and 101 steps. In addition to the lighthouse, there are keeper's dwellings of wood and a brick oil house. While the architect is unknown, the builder was Phoenix Ironworks, Ocean City, New Jersey.

Lighting devices are on display at Sanibel Historical Village and Museum. Consult Appendix A and verify hours before making the trip. The lighthouse is not open to the public, although the grounds about it are.

DIRECTIONS

From I-75 in south Ft. Myers, exit west on Daniels Parkway and follow the numerous directional signs to Sanibel. Once past Punta Rassa, an event the visitor may not even notice, cross the causeway (stopping to pay a presently $6 toll), and come to the stop sign, turn left or south and proceed to the public beach, pier, and lighthouse.

IMPORTANT DATES

1833 First Sanibel Settlers
1836 Second-Seminole War Forces Settlers to Leave
1837 Fort Delaney Established at Punta Rassa
1883 Lighthouse Board Approves Lighthouse
1884 Lighthouse Built
1923 Lighted by Acetylene Gas
1944 Residents Shelter from Hurricane in Lighthouse
1948 Damaged by Hurricane
1949 Automated
1962 Lighthouse Electrified
1967 Sanibel Wildlife Refuge Named in Honor of J. N. "Ding" Darling
1974 Lighthouse Placed on the National Register of Historic Places
2004 Hurricane Charley

Sanibel Island Lighthouse

To Sarasota

FORT MYERS

Pine Island

Captiva Island

Cape Coral

Sanibel Island

Ft. Myers Beach

Gulf of Mexico

To Naples

75 · 41 · 867 · 867 · 869

SHELTER FROM THE STORM

On Friday the 13th in August, 2004, Hurricane Charley made a right hook onto Sanibel and Captiva islands as it approached Punta Gorda, where the devastation was horrible.

Despite numerous warnings to evacuate, a number of people stayed on the barrier islands when Charley struck. They were fortunately spared by the speed of the hurricane and the small size of its eye, both of which diminished the storm surge. Hurricane Charley's forecast storm surge of 13 feet never materialized. It is estimated the surge reached only 6 feet. This was still a substantial surge for islands like Sanibel, where the average elevation might be 4 feet. Had the storm moved more slowly and the eye had been the predicted 10 miles across, instead of 5, even more massive destruction could have occurred.

This was not the first hurricane to threaten the barrier islands. In 1944, 40 people took shelter from another awesome hurricane by huddling on the spiral steps of Sanibel Lighthouse. That storm had peak winds of 163 miles-per-hour. The attack of the wind and surf in such a small structure must have been frightening. There was no bridge to the mainland until the early 1960s, so island residents and lighthouse keepers were pretty much on their own.

SMITH SHOAL LIGHT
(Monroe County)

One of the screw-pile lighthouses built to be unmanned, little is known of Smith Shoal Light. The Coast Guard describes it as a hexagonal, pyramidal, skeleton tower with a height of 54 feet. Its white light flashes every 6 seconds and can be seen at a distance of 9 miles. This light, built in 1933, is rarely mentioned in print. Smith Shoal is northwest of Key West and a long ways from anything.

SOMBRERO KEY LIGHTHOUSE
(Monroe County)

Standing 156 feet, Sombrero Key Lighthouse is the tallest of the screw-pile lighthouses and went into action before the Civil War. The lighthouse has withstood nearly 150 years of storms, and lasted several generations of puny humans.

Sombrero, of course, is Spanish for a type of wide-brimmed hat. It is possible that the name is related to the perceived shape of the reef. Historian Gail Swanson reports that Sombrero Key is one of Florida's oldest place names but its origin is unknown. In 1743, a Spanish priest, Father Joseph X. Alana, was on a mission to convert the pagan Native Americans of Tequesta (Miami), when he drew a map of the area with the name Sombrero Key.

Sombrero Key Lighthouse was the last of the screw-piles built by then Captain George Meade. He intended to build Rebecca Shoal Lighthouse, but a hurricane took down that work in progress and the Civil War intervened, taking Meade to greater glory. Sombrero Key, lies between the two lights of Carysfort and Sand Key, also built by Meade.

Sombrero Key and Reef are located in an area of vigorous seas and currents, and like most of the Keys, has reefs that can be difficult to see in the dark or where the water is turbulent. From Overseas Highway and with good eyesight, the lighthouse can be clearly seen in the Atlantic from Seven Mile Bridge.

In 1960, Hurricane Donna blew mightily at the lighthouse with winds recorded at 200 miles-per-hour. The Coast Guard personnel on board were barely evacuated. The lighthouse received major damage and had to be extensively repaired. Not the first time either, as a hurricane in August of 1856 stopped work on it when it was under construction. In that hurricane, the partially completed lighthouse was destroyed and had to be built again.

Sombrero Key is now automated, and

its old lens sits in the Key West Lighthouse Museum. The lighthouse had a fixed, first-order Fresnel lens.

An annual Sombrero Cup Regatta is held around Sombrero Key. The cup started in the 1980s and has become a tradition.

Currently, a Vega VRB-25 Beacon rotates, putting forth a white group of flashes every 60 seconds, with three red sectors. The focal plane is 142 feet. With Lieutenant George Meade as Chief Engineer, the lighthouse was built by I. P. Morris and Company, of Philadelphia, Pennsylvania. The architect is unknown, but the Fresnel lens was manufactured by Henri-LePuate.

DIRECTIONS

Sombrero Reef lies a few miles offshore of Marathon in the Atlantic Ocean. Diving and fishing around Sombrero are popular, as at most of the offshore lighthouses.

IMPORTANT DATES

1856 Hurricane Delays Construction
1858 Lighthouse Built
1912 Incandescent Oil Vapor Lamp
1931 Light Changed to Flashing and Revolving Beacon
1939 Civilian Keepers Replaced by Coast Guard Personnel
1960 Lighthouse Damaged by Hurricane Donna, Lighthouse Automated
1980 Alligator Reef, American Shoal, and Sombrero Key Used as Outposts in Mariel Boat Lift
1982 First-order Lens Removed to Key West Lighthouse Museum. Vega VRB-25 Rotating Beacon Installed.
(Also given in print as 1983 and 1984)

Sombrero Key Lighthouse

Marathon

VACA KEY

Atlantic Ocean

TENNESSEE REEF LIGHT
(Monroe County)

Located south of Long Key, Tennessee Reef Light is a small, screw-pile lighthouses designed to be operated unmanned. It is described as hexagonal, pyramidal, skeletal, and lacked keeper's quarters.

The light was built on Tennessee Reef in 1933 with a height of 49 feet from mean high water to the focal plane. That, of course, is the Coast Guard height, although different sources give other heights. The pattern was white flashes every 4 seconds.

It is likely that Tennessee Reef is named for a vessel lost on September 8, 1832, which wrecked on Long Key.

TIERRA VERDE LIGHTHOUSE
(Pinellas County)

This latest, official aid to navigation was built by Tampa Bay Watch, and it is sometimes also referred to as the Tampa Bay Watch Lighthouse. It has as its primary purpose aiding navigation when the weather is stormy. It is not the primary light in the area; that distinction goes to Egmont Key. Nonetheless, it is remarkable and encouraging to think of a brand-new lighthouse for this century.

It has a 155-mm optic and a plastic Fresnel lens. It is lighted by a 0.55 amp light inside the clear lens. The focal plane is at 64 feet above mean sea level. To the top of the lightning arrestor is 70 feet. It sits atop Tampa Bay Watch Marine Center, a building containing education and management offices for the organization.

Tampa Bay Watch is a fine organization with the admirable goal of restoring the health of Tampa Bay, including direct restoration and education. The organization was founded in 1992 and patterned on the Hudson Riverkeeper, an organization formed to protect the Hudson River.

Among Tampa Bay Watch's many projects are restoration of lost saltwater wetlands and sea grasses. It has helped oyster beds to flourish and used artificial reefs to promote fishery health. It works closely with the Tampa Bay National Estuary Program.

Since the 1950s when the health of Tampa Bay was first documented, at least 50% of the sea grasses and mangroves have disappeared. The bay, once rich is scallops, is now a hard place to find one. Oyster production dropped sharply also. The primary causes of this were: enrichment from sewage and storm-water runoff, and development, including dredging and outright destruction of mangroves. Other

impairments came from industrial accidents, including acidic spills from phosphate processing and unenlightened sewage processing. The bay is at least holding its own, maybe improving, and this is due in large part to efforts of both the Tampa Bay Watch and the National Estuary Program.

Contacts for Tampa Bay Watch can be found in Appendix A. The Education Center is open to the public and visitors are welcome.

DIRECTIONS
The Light is located at the Marine Center at Bunces Pass at the entrance into Fort DeSoto Park. From I-275 in St. Petersburg, take the last southern exit before the Skyway Bridge and follow the signs.

Top: Tierra Verde Lighthouse as seen from across the channel. An official aid to navigation, it assists Egmont Key Light in guiding ships into Tampa Bay. The lighthouse is atop the new center for Tampa Bay Watch, an organization devoted to protecting the health of Tampa Bay.

Above: A grand opening is in progress for the lighthouse and the new education center for Tampa Bay Watch.

Opposite page: Two views of Sombrero Key Lighthouse.

BEACONS

The heart of a lighthouse is its lamp or beacon. In the history of lighthouses, there have been several methods of creating the light, such as the multi-wick lamp shown at middle right, and modern sources such as the Vega Beacon at near right and the 300mm drum light, at far right, bottom. The related technology is the method of focusing and amplifying the light. This technology reached a peak of craftsmanship and artistry with the beautiful glass prism array of the first-0order Fresnel lens at top, left. At top, right, is a less powerful, but equally beautiful, fourth-order Fresnel lens.

BEACONS

At top, a view of a first order Fresnel lens, opened for maintenance. At right, a view of the "bullseye" lenses which are at the heart of the Fresnel design, surrounded by prisms. Above, a third order Fresnel with simulated lighting.

TRIUMPH REEF LIGHT
(Monroe County)

Only 19 feet tall, Triumph Reef is barely mentioned in print. If not for a reference in Love Dean's excellent book, *Lighthouses of the Florida Keys*, it might not have been included at all. That reference is that Hurricane Andrew ran right over it in 1992 (and likely washed over it too).

Triumph Reef Light is located miles from anywhere, south of Fowey Rocks and north of Carysfort. It is triangle-shaped and set on a set of piles that connect at the top, like teepee poles, called a dolphin. The light is red every 2.5 seconds. Other than that, little is known about it.

Neil Hurley notes that in 1933, Triumph Reef was an unlighted beacon. In 1951, it was recorded as a unlighted buoy. It was a lighted buoy between 1968 and 1977, and was a light before 1982.

VOLUSIA BAR LIGHTHOUSE
(Volusia County, destroyed)

Lake George is Florida's second-largest lake after Okeechobee, but, calling either of them lakes is a little misleading. Okeechobee, mother to the Everglades, is an impoundment, encircled by a dike in modern times. Lake George is just a wide spot in the St. Johns River.

With wind and storms, whitecaps are a common sight on Lake George. Fogs are also common, and the lighthouse built in the southern reaches of Lake George had a fog bell. In the late 1800s, when the lighthouse was built, river transportation was the primary means of supply. Overland travel was slow. Work began in 1885 and the lighthouse was operational in March 1886. The 49-foot lighthouse was built in relatively shallow waters and had a focal plane of 38 feet. It was a white, wooden building, with iron piles. It was lighted at first with a fourth-order Fresnel lens, and later with a fifth-order lens, and cast a fixed white light. Although it was deactivated in 1916, it remained standing to help navigators with the fogs.

The lighthouse was abandoned in 1943. The lighthouse was destroyed by vandals who set a fire in 1970. The piles remain. They can be reached by boat from the Volusia Bar Boat Ramp at the end of Zinder Point. SR-40 is the predominate road in the area. It meets both I-95 and I-75. From SR-40 approximately 5-miles west of the St. Johns, turn north on Blue Creek Lodge Road. A sign, if still standing, will show within a mile or so, the way to the boat landing.

HB

Top: Volusia Bar Lighthouse

IMPORTANT DATES
1885 Construction Begins
1886 Lighthouse Lighted (March)
1916 Deactivated
1943 Station Abandoned
1970 Destroyed

ANOTHER LAKE LIGHTHOUSE
The town of Mount Dora claims a lighthouse. Mount Dora overlooks Lake Dora. This lighthouse is merely decorative and has no function. The town of Mount Dora is located at the approximate western dead-end of SR-46, just north of Orlando.

SB

APPENDIX A

Associations, Clubs, Organizations, Parks, and Refuges

Anclote Key State Park
Gulf Islands GeoPark
#1 Causeway Blvd.
Dunedin FL 34698
727-893-2627

Amelia Island Museum
109 South 18th Street
Fernandina Beach FL 32034

Anastasia Island State Park
1340A A1A South
St. Augustine FL 32084
904-461-2033
www.myflorida.com

Bahia Honda State Park
36850 Overseas Highway
Big Pine Key FL 33043
305-872-3897

Barrier Island Parks Society
PO Box 637 Boca Grande FL 33921
941-964-0060
941-964-0054 (fax)

Bill Baggs Cape Florida State Park
1200 South Crandon Blvd.
Key Biscayne FL 33149
305-361-5811
305-365-0003 (fax)
www.floridaparks.org/capeflorida

Biscayne National Park
PO Box 1369
Homestead FL 33090
305-230-7275
www.nps.gov/bisc
concession: 305-230-1100

Canaveral National Seashore
308 Julia St.
Titusville FL 32796
407-267-1110

Cape Canaveral Lighthouse Foundation
PO Box 1978
Cape Canaveral FL 32920
www.capecanaverallighthousefoundation
.com
phones 407-494-5959, 407-494-5949

Cape St. George Lighthouse Society, Inc.
PO Box 915
Apalachicola FL 32329

Carrabelle Lighthouse Association
PO Box 373
Carrabelle FL 32322
crkdrvrlh@aol.com

Cayo Costa State Park
PO Box 1150
Boca Grande FL 33921
941-964-0375
www.myflorida.com

Cedar Key Historical Museum and Cedar Key Historical Society
PO Box 222
Cedar Key FL 32626

Cedar Key Museum State Park
12231 SW 166 Court
Cedar Key FL 32625
352-543-5350
www.floridastateparks.org

Cedar Keys National Wildlife Refuge
16450 NW 31st Place
Chiefland FL 32626
352-493-0238
352-493-1935 (fax)
www.cedarkeys.fws.gov

Crooked River Lighthouse Association
PO Box 373
Carrabelle FL 32322

"Ding" Darling National Wildlife Refuge
1 Wildlife Drive
Sanibel FL 33957
239-472-1100

Dry Tortugas National Park
PO Box 6208
Key West FL 33041
305-242-7700

Egmont Key Alliance
PO Box 66238
St. Petersburg Beach FL 33736
www.egmontkey.org

Egmont Key State Park
Gulf Islands GeoPark
#1 Causeway Blvd.
Dunedin FL 34698
727-893-2627

Florida Keys National Marine Sanctuary
PO Box 500368
Marathon FL 33050
305-743-2437
305-743-2357 (fax)
www.fknms.nos.noaa.gov

Florida Keys National Wildlife Refuges
PO Box 43050
Big Pine Key FL 33043
305-872-0774

Florida Keys Reef Lighthouse Foundation, Inc.
PO Box 504442
Marathon FL 33050
www.floridalighthouses.org/reeflights

Florida Lighthouse Association
PO Box 340028
Tampa FL 33694
www.floridalighthouses.org

Fort Clinch State Park
2601 Atlantic Avenue
Fernandina Beach FL 32034
904-277-7274
www.myflorida.com

Gasparilla Island Maritime Museum
PO Box 100
Boca Grande FL 33921

Gasparilla Island State Park
PO Box 1150
Boca Grande FL 32921
941-964-0375
www.FloridaStateParks.org/
gasparillaisland

Gulf Islands National Seashore
1801 Gulf Breeze Parkway
Gulf Breeze FL 32561
850-934-2600

Hillsboro Lighthouse Preservation Society, Inc.
PO Box 6062
Pompano Beach FL 33060
954-782-3313
www.HillsboroLighthouse.org

Historical Museum of Southern Florida
101 West Flagler Street
Miami FL 33130
305-375-1492
305-375-1609 (fax)

Indian Key State Historic Site
PO Box 1052
Islamorada FL 33036
305-664-2540

Jonathan Dickinson State Park
16540 Southeast Federal Highway
Hobe Sound FL 33455
561-546-2772
www.myflorida.com

John Pennekamp Coral Reef State Park
PO Box 487
Key Largo FL 33037
305-451-1410
www.myflorida.com

Jupiter Inlet Lighthouse
805 North US-1
Jupiter FL 33477
404-747-8380

Key West Art And Historical Society, Inc.
281 Front Street
Key West FL 33040
305-295-6616
www.kwhs.com/lighthouse.htm

Key West Lighthouse Museum
938 Whitehead Street
Key West FL 33040
305-294-0012

Lignumvitae Key Botanical State Park
PO Box 1052
Islamorada FL 33036
305-664-2540

Lower Suwannee National Wildlife Refuge
16450 NW 31st Place
Chiefland FL 32626
352-493-0238
www.lowersuwannee.fws.gov

Mayport Naval Air Station
PO Box 280032
Naval Station Mayport FL 32228-0032

Merritt Island National Wildlife Refuge
PO Box 6504
Titusville FL 32782
407-861-0662

Pensacola Naval Air Station
190 Radford Blvd.
Pensacola FL 32508

Ponce de Leon Inlet Light Station Ponce de Leon Inlet Lighthouse Museum
4931 South Peninsula Drive
Ponce Inlet FL 32127
386-761-1821
386-761-3121 (fax)
www.ponceinlet.org

St. Augustine Lighthouse and Museum
81 Lighthouse Avenue
St. Augustine FL 32084
904-829-0745
904-829-3144 (fax)
www.stauglight.com

St. George Island State Park
1900 E. Gulf Beach Ave.
St. George Island FL 32338
850-927-2111

St. George Light House Association, Inc.
201 Bradford Street
St. George Island FL 32328
www.stgeorgelight.org

St. Joseph Bay Aquatic Preserve
350 Carroll Street
Eastpoint FL 32328
850-227-1327

St. Joseph Historical Society
PO Box 231
Port St. Joe FL 32457

St. Joseph Peninsula State Park
8899 Cape San Blas Road
Port St. Joe FL 32456
850-227-1327

St. Marks National Wildlife Refuge
Box 68
St. Marks FL 32355
850-925-6121

St. Vincents National Wildlife Refuge
PO Box 447
Apalachicola FL 32329
850-663-8808

Sanibel/Captiva Chamber of Commerce
Causeway Road
Sanibel FL 33957

Sanibel Historical Village and Museum
950 Dunlop Road
Sanibel FL 33957
239-472-4648

Tampa Bay Watch, Inc.
3000 Pinellas Bay Way South
Tierre Verde FL 33715
727-867-8166
727-867-8188 (fax)
www.TampaBayWatch.org

Florida Lighthouse Books and
Reference Material

*A Light in the Wilderness: The Story of
Jupiter Inlet Lighthouse & the Southeast
Florida Frontier* by James D. Snyder,
available from Pharos Books

Bansemer's Book of Florida Lighthouses,
Roger Bansemer, Pineapple Press

"Big Diamond," Newsletter of the
Hillsboro Lighthouse Preservation
Society, Inc.

*"First Light: The Story of the St.
Augustine Lighthouse,"* Video Tape,
East Coast Marketing, Available from
St. Augustine Lighthouse and Museum

"Florida Flash," Quarterly Newsletter of
the Florida Lighthouse Association, Inc.

Florida Lighthouses for Kids,
Elinor D. Wire, Pineapple Press

Florida Lighthouse Trails,
Thomas Taylor, Editor, Pineapple Press

Florida Place Names,
Joan Perry Morris, Pineapple Press

Florida's Lighthouses, Kevin McCarthy,
University of Florida Press

Florida's Lighthouses in the Civil War,
Neil Hurley, Middle River Press

*Florida's Territorial Lighthouses:
1821-1845,* Thomas Taylor, Florida
Sesquicentennial Publications

*Gulf Coast Lighthouses: Florida Keys
to the Rio Grande,* Roberts and Jones,
Globe Pequot Press.

Guardians of the Lights,
Elinor De Wire, Pineapple Press

Guide to Florida Lighthouses,
Elinor De Wire, Pineapple Press

Hillsboro Lighthouse, David F. Butler,
Pompano Beach Historical Society

*Keepers of Florida Lighthouses:
1820-1939,* Neil Hurley, Historic
Lighthouse Publishers

*Lighthouses, Lightships, and the Gulf
of Mexico,* David Cipra, Cypress
Communications

Lighthouses of the Dry Tortugas,
Neil Hurley, Historical Lighthouse
Publishers

Lighthouses of the Florida Keys,
Love Dean, Pineapple Press

*"Pinpoint Guide to Florida
Lighthouses,"* Crane Hill Publishers

*"Timeline of the St. Augustine
Lighthouse,"* available from
St. Augustine Lighthouse and Museum

*St. Augustine Lighthouse: A Short
History,* Rosalinda Lind, available from
St. Augustine Lighthouse and Museum

*1994 Inventory of Historic Light
Stations,* National Maritime Initiative,
National Park Service

DECORATIVE LIGHTHOUSES

Faro Blanco, a hotel and marina in the Keys, is one of several buildings in Florida which have taken the iconic and historic "look" of lighthouse architecture and used it for a commercial purpose which is totally unrelated to the navigation of ships although the "lighthouse" does help a mariner find the marina.